Love, Not Guns

Love, Not Guns

A Case For Changing the Focus of America's Gun Debate

Published by M&B Global Solutions Inc.
United States of America (USA)

Love, Not Guns

*A Case For Changing the Focus
of America's Gun Debate*

Jay Breitlow, D.C.

Love, Not Guns

Contents

Dedicated to my father,
Dale Breitlow

Preface

I wrote this book because I believe we can all make a difference in saving and enhancing the lives of not just our children, but people around the world. I am an expert in school-related violence not by choice or research, but because of personal experience.

December 1, 1993: While in class as a freshman at Wauwatosa West High School in Wauwatosa, Wisconsin, our associate principal was shot and killed. This entire event shook our community, and I was one of thousands of students who would walk the halls in which his life was taken.

However, it shook our family a little more, as the associate principal, Dale Breitlow, was also my hero. He was my father.

Writing this book, researching, re-researching and going back to that tragic day time and again has been extremely difficult for me, yet at the same time therapeutic. This is an extraordinarily personal book, and a look into what it feels like to be the person "this could never happen to."

In talking about this subject often, I realize I am talking about things that are often socially, spiritually and certainly politically charged. Yet it is my hope and deepest desire that the thoughts contained in this book will save at least one life and create a new thread of conversation.

I hope this book becomes the impetus for change in how we treat everyone from the mentally ill to the perceived healthy; from the school nerd to the athletics star. The day this book is no longer relevant is a day for us all to rejoice, as it means we have created a tangible change in schools and playgrounds everywhere.

I believe school-related violence, and violence in general, is a real-life problem that has answers. However, I believe the questions we are currently asking don't have solutions. I believe that many of the answers for protecting our schools lie directly in the questions themselves. Merely asking the following question puts into motion the foundation for the solution: "How can I create more love?"

Most people don't have the time or resources to create a platform for global change. Most people are not president of the United States or the mayor of New York City. But that doesn't mean you lack the ability to create change.

In fact, I believe it means the opposite, in that you have just as much – if not more – direct power in shaping your community. It is far more likely that your neighbor will have influence on you or your family than anybody you see on TV, and vice versa!

For decades, the United States has struggled with keeping schools safe for our innocent and loved. Despite law after law and one new safety precaution after another, the violence and death toll rises. Why?

I will explore all sides of the most common and current questions being asked, and talk about why they inherently fail to find answers.

The only thing people seem to agree upon is that a safe and healthy environment for education is paramount to the success of our communities. So why aren't we focusing on the one thing that binds us all together: love?

Love holds the answer to all our questions when you ask the questions the correct way.

I'm not talking about creating a 1960s hippie revolution all over again, although that might not hurt. What I do suggest are practical ways to help your children, neighbors and total strangers. I also look at ways to appropriate energy and finances in our society to further human development, potential and health.

I conducted most, if not all, of my research with the exact same technology you have at your fingertips: the internet. We are truly at a wonderful time in human evolution where facts, as well as misconceptions, can run as fast as your megaphone is loud. My challenge was to look at every question at every angle and figure out, "When is talking about love not an answer?" I feel that in the end, nobody can have more connection with what is at stake than me as a husband, son and father. I stand by all research, questions and answers in this book.

The best part of technology today is that by typing in one simple keyword from anywhere in the world, I can pull up the April 24, 1994, late edition of the *Milwaukee Journal* for details about my father's killing. Through Facebook, I was able to contact classmates of my father's killer as well as my father's colleagues. Because let's be honest, when I was fifteen, my life and memories were vastly different than they are now.

Since I lost my father, I have struggled to identify with the people who want to ban or limit guns in our communities. I have also struggled to identify with people who want more guns in our communities. I have enrolled in gun safety classes to attempt to connect with one side of the gun conversation, only to feel pulled back to the other side and be the class no-show.

Then one day, a friend of mine asked me if I would consider giving a talk at our local Rotary Club about gun violence. She knew my experience made me somewhat of an expert and that it would be a powerful talk if I would accept. I told her I would think about it, and I internally debated if I really wanted to be back in the public eye again, even if it was just a hundred local friends.

Then while talking with my aforementioned friend and life coach, Dr. Tom Preston, he helped me see that I could talk on this topic, but that my answer was different then just "yes or no" to guns. You see, I can't identify with either side, or even be in the middle of the conversation with guns because that is not a conversation that ultimately provides answers.

Year after year, month after month, seeing the headlines on the news about the latest school shooting, you might be like me in thinking: "Well, there is no answer." Yet the fight goes on and on. One state has different rules; one senator wants to change federal laws; one mayor wants more background checks; one city wants guns in the hands of every resident; one president wants different laws than another. It seems as if there won't ever be a consensus.

Then one day, it came out in a conversation with Dr. Tom that the answer I was seeking was different than the questions people were asking. The reason why there is no answer to the gun debate is because it's the wrong question. There is no loving answer to a question that centers on implements of death and destruction.

The better question, in my opinion, is: How do we solve violence in America? And that answer is with love!

Chapter 1

Our Back Story

This book is a story about our family. It's a story not about our pains and losses, but about the depths of love and how love heals all; a story that I hope genuinely enriches and changes your life to revolve around love, both for the good times and the difficult times.

I am the eldest of the two sons born to Dale and Sue Breitlow. The best way for me to describe how we were brought up is to say simply: We were loved.

And we continue to be. To this day, my mother loves us and her four grandchildren more than anything in the world.

For fifteen years of my life, I had the love of two amazing parents. But on December 1, 1993, my father – also my high school's associate principal – was shot in a hallway I would walk for another three-and-a-half years.

If you have picked up this book, no doubt you have been through tough times. My relationship with Ty, my younger brother by two-and-a-half years, is no exception. My brother and I were best friends (usually) and despite some otherwise rocky brotherly crises, we really had the best of all worlds. Perhaps most importantly, we provide balance in each other's lives. I don't know that I could have gone through the process of losing my father alone. Having a younger brother to share in the tough times just seemed to help – even if we never talked about it.

Sometimes there was a sense of "I need to be strong for my brother and mother," and other times, when I was down in the dumps, I would look at Ty and say to myself, "If he can do it, you can make it another day." It was almost like an unwritten code.

The love we received in our lives went well beyond our parents, as our

grandparents spoiled us with love as well – all four of them! Not spoiled rotten, yet we knew where the cookie drawer was and that Santa always came on Christmas. It was common knowledge that every time we went to "the farm," (our slang for the area my parents grew up in) spoils were a-comin'.

For Ty and me, our father-and-sons bonding experiences revolved round sports. My father seemingly had a one-track mind with these missions: Make these events a more frequent occurrence. The only

My dad with me at age 6

problem was my father was consistently torn between advancing his career in education and moves that took our family farther from Milwaukee. He eventually accepted a demotion for the sole purpose of moving closer to the big city.

This was my dad's dream, live somewhere the Brewers played baseball in the summer, the Bucks played basketball in the winter and the Green Bay Packers would play a few times in the fall (through 1994). My father loved all these teams, and I was raised to speak of them in reverence when times were good and in hope when times were bad.

I was born and raised to the age of eight near Madison, Wisconsin, in the city of Cambridge. This was great for watching big-time college football games and close enough to Milwaukee, but my father's career in Cambridge likely wouldn't speedily evolve beyond high school teacher. So we ended up following the job trail, moving to the rural city of Montello and eventually to the Milwaukee suburb of Wauwatosa. But before we get to the big city, let's rewind …

Sue DeLain and Dale Breitlow grew up in two unincorporated Wisconsin farming towns about three miles apart. Sue was the second eldest of twelve brothers and sisters, and Dale was the youngest of three. The largest town was about twenty miles away in the industrial city of Green Bay.

Green Bay isn't a huge city by any stretch of the imagination, but Euren, where my mom grew up, had about two dozen residents, if you take out the dozen DeLain brothers and sisters. No typo, friends, Mom's hometown has been at the front and back end of punch lines as long as I can remember. And yes, it's pronounced like urine.

Rio Creek was about the same, but a feed mill in town would keep the city of Rio Creek a bit busier through the year. The total population of around four dozen generally was achieved when everybody had family and friends over to watch Green Bay Packers football games on TV.

Life was simple growing up in a part of the world where the major source of revenue revolved around farming. Well, farming *and* the Packers. My dad lived on a farm with a natural artesian spring. Thus, the name "The

Breitlow Overflowing Well Dairy Farm" was painted prominently on the farm silo.

The DeLain family didn't grow up directly on a farm, although the

My parents' high school homecoming photo

family did own a sizeable amount of land. Instead, Vince DeLain Sr. was the local bovine artificial inseminator. In this part of the world, if you weren't a farmer, you contributed to the farm trade in another way.

Life just moved at a different pace in the mid-twentieth century. Everybody knew everybody, and unless you did something pretty rotten to your neighbors, everybody helped one another. My mom and dad's families knew each other, and often times, families in this area knew each other's business – for better or worse. My parents met for the first time in high school and became friends. What started as a simple friendship soon blossomed into much more.

Dale Breitlow and Sue DeLain were high school sweethearts, eventually becoming homecoming king and queen at Casco High School. They were best friends, and as their families were already well-acquainted and lived a short distance apart, it didn't take long for them to turn into trouble makers. Thumbing through my parents' old high school yearbook one lonely Sunday afternoon when I was in high school, I read about it first-hand.

I learned how one night my dad "borrowed" the farm car and drove the three miles to Euren for a late-night rendezvous of star gazing and beer drinking. Later that night, the roads became icy and the couple ended up in the ditch a little too young and a little too drunk for their situation. With few others on the road, they walked to a friend's house and enlisted his help in pulling them out of the ditch so they could safely return the car before the sun came up.

Among my other nosy adventures, I later learned that long-distance college writing became a frequent communication venture for them. This was the first time space had come between my parents. My father ended up at Wisconsin State (now known as the University of Wisconsin-Oshkosh) and my mother at Bellin School of Nursing (now Bellin College) in Green Bay.

The staggering fifty miles for young sweethearts was not enough to keep their love from growing, though. I literally found dozens of saved letters from when my parents were in college. At that time (my wife would tell you to this day) I didn't know you weren't supposed to read such things! I was intrigued.

I did find one letter from my mother to my father, a less-than-excited one that stood out in particular. I guess fifty miles isn't enough to keep a rumor from circulating. The letter basically said that my mother had heard through the grapevine that Dad had gone out with another woman to a dance. Well, knowing my jovial, well-intentioned father, he probably thought nothing of it – and certainly never expected it would get back to his love.

"Dale, I heard you went with Janie to the ball last week. I am writing to let you know that I am seeing Tommy now."

I asked my mother about that letter. She told me she couldn't understand what he was thinking: "I mean, Dale lived in a house with so many mutual friends. Do you remember the Critters, honey?" I responded that I did. The Critters were a clique of a dozen or so close-knit friends in college who lived and partied together. They continued to do so well after college, staying in contact to this date.

My mother continued with the story and told me that one of the Critters saw him get the letter, "and he went from excitement straight to misery." When the guys asked him what the letter said, they received a surprising response: He said nothing. He dropped his head.

"When he found out I was going to date other people, that was the end of that," my mom said with a sly grin. "I don't think he ever dated another woman again. He only had eyes for me."

Obviously, things worked out in the end, as four years later they were married right down the road from where they grew up. I can only imagine the party that was had that night by the Breitlows and DeLains. The wedding photos show a beautiful, dark-haired woman smiling politely and pretty for the camera, hand-in-hand with the groom. The groom and his tall, big-boned body was a strong and protective presence next to her.

The striking thing about the wedding photos to me is that I can tell they are both so very much in love. Seeing my father, with his oversized glasses and giant red sideburns smiling ear-to-ear, reminds me how he commanded such a presence; yet he was always easy to speak to. With a booming laugh that appeared frequently, you could just tell he was the life of the party.

Rarely in a wedding photo does the groom overshadow the bride. But for me, looking at my father in that picture, he was larger than life.

I don't know what the perfect family looks like to others, but I know that my life growing up was with the perfect family. Ty and I were loved by our parents. We were nurtured in a loving, yet disciplined environment, with a stern respect for right and wrong. When we misbehaved, there were always two consequences: The red imprint of my father's hand on my white rear end and this disappointment that you let your hero down.

Yes, spankings sucked, and as much as my father insisted, "This is going to hurt me more than it hurts you," I couldn't fathom what he meant. Only now that I have a daughter can I begin to understand how much love he had in his heart.

I hope I never have to spank Selom, but at the same time I can now appreciate the tough, yet thoughtful and purposeful love my father gave me growing up.

Dad's lifelong ambition was in the arena of education, and he was not good at it. He was great. After playing football and baseball in college at Wisconsin State, he graduated with a teaching degree. Shortly thereafter, he was hired to be the biology teacher and basketball coach at Cambridge High School just outside Madison.

How ironic was it that my mother was hired for her first job as a nurse at a veteran's hospital in Madison? One would think they were just meant to be, weren't they? My mother retired in 2014 to a standing ovation. She had been well-respected in her profession for over four decades. She finished her career in the same hospital she started after moving from one VA to the next as our family evolved.

We had a magnificent life in Cambridge. To this day, I can still remember the joys of the unknown objects Dad would bring home from school each week: aquatic plants, exotic fish, toads, tadpoles or reptiles. These remnants of high school experiments were highlights of my early childhood.

One day I learned that Dad had decided to "go back to school," which never made sense in my head. Wasn't he already at school every day? The man who taught other students had something left to learn? How could this be? How can anyone teach my father anything? I mean, he was so far up on that pedestal I put him on … absurd!

Turns out the reason we took the half-hour drive into Madison on the weekends was not just for the kickass zoo and ice cream at Ella's Deli and Ice Cream Parlor. Indeed, the man was taking classes working toward his MBA at the University of Wisconsin-Madison. While mom, Ty and I were off exploring the world of zebras and merry-go-rounds, he was working his butt off to advance his career.

The routine was to get up, drive into town and drop Dad off at this big, fancy concrete building in clearly the biggest town we had ever seen, with his hard-cover leather briefcase. It should be noted here that many people throughout history have used briefcases, but how many live with their briefcase? Dad rarely left the house without his papers from the office neatly organized into a hard, brown leather case, complete with pens, paperclips, index cards and the daily sports page.

To this day, my wife asks me why I take my laptop bag with me, oh, everywhere. And yes, everywhere does include the beach, the mountains and sometimes church. All I can do is shrug and say, "My father did it."

While we are on the list of peculiar habits my father passed down to his son, let me mention the always-trusty "index card in breast pocket" routine. The reason why I frequently carry index cards is my father used to create a daily to-do list, carrying it with him all day. You would think my dad was a connoisseur of fine three-by-five-inch narrow-ruled index cards. The fact he was a public school teacher and had a limitless supply, well, that just added fuel to the fire.

My father could be seen adding an idea to the list or a name to call later at any moment in time. He kind of resembled a soccer referee at a World Cup game. You know the routine: the referee gives a yellow card, pulling out their notebook of names and notes to remember. Same idea.

Our family loved the all-you-can-eat fish fry common in Wisconsin. A typical Friday evening would find us gorging ourselves on cod and perch. Back in the pre-cellphone days, it wasn't uncommon for someone to ask my father for directions to the nearest gas station. *Whap.* Out of the breast pocket comes a newly minted index card. After a couple laughs, sometimes a drink, and a dissertation about gas station options, the destination was set. Complete with a hand drawn map and a list of turns, the fellow would be off to the nearest 7-Eleven.

The funny thing about my dad is these random conversations would often lead to friendships. Thinking nothing of it, Dad would just put his name and number on the card and say, "Give me a ring next time you are in town. We've got an extra bed." Famously, we attracted a lifelong friend in this way, except this guy my dad met in an airport. To this day, we still keep in contact with him.

I'm not sure how the market is for principals nowadays, but back in 1986, job openings were few and far between. As luck would have it, when you are a big, tall man with a gift for the jovial, people remember you.

The job Dad ended up getting was out of an application pool of several hundred well-qualified and more-tenured peers. The only problem was it was smack-dab in the middle of the state, in the tiny town of Montello, close to nowhere in particular. Knowing full well that this job was a stepping stone to getting to the big city, our stop in Montello was a short four years.

Many times, my mother has asserted, "We should have never left Cambridge." Oftentimes she makes the statement out of the blue. I have given that idea some scrutiny as time has passed. I believe that when the end result is losing a family member, it's natural to look at what brought you here or blame the place geographically.

When I'm honest with myself, there were definitely signs from the universe – God, if you will – that could have pointed us right back to Cambridge, or at least staying nearby. One such sign is when my father got the job in Montello, we had to commute until we had a place to live.

The trip was about ninety minutes each way and required us leaving Cambridge in a rusty Montello School District van. Picture an A-Team type van, except with no seats in the back. I think my father may have done this part by design and taken the seats out himself. This man brought in heaps of pillows, sheets and comforters for us to sleep during the early-morning journey to Montello every Monday.

I guess it wasn't so bad for us, but for my dad, leaving the house at 5 a.m. and being the zombie driver across the state, well, that probably wasn't awesome. I'm also not entirely sure he didn't know that there was a rusty hole in the bottom of the van, but I didn't mind it. I could tell just how far we were by the amount of daylight that shone through that hole.

(L-r) Me, my mom, Ty and my dad

It's not like the move to Montello created a huge amount of familial hardship. I know there are people without houses and without parents out there. Really, the entire situation just added to our family stress. Part of the reason for commuting like this was to give us time to find our perfect house, after all. Anybody who has ever moved knows there can be a fantastic amount of stress involved with selling the old house and timing it right with a new one. That timing wasn't perfect for our family, either; hence the wannabe mini-van excursions in the rusted A-Team van.

Montello was great once we got settled in. My parents decided that the best place for our growing family was a log cabin-style house set back off a big fishing lake. You heard that right. We spent the next four years living in a log cabin, in the woods by a lake. It was great, and even included a pool across the street! A real life, in-ground swimming pool! It was almost like living on perpetual summer vacation.

The little community we lived in was full of Wisconsin snowbirds. This meant the majority of people would show up in April or May, stay until October and then head south for the winter. Just like summer vacation, each season came to an end. The winters were cold and desolate.

Our log cabin was big and spacious, not the type of cabin Walter White holed up in during the last season of the show "Breaking Bad." It was, for us, a mansion in the woods.

The house had electric baseboard heating, but we rarely used it. Instead, my parents preferred to heat the house via a giant wood stove in the family room. The problem was twofold: splitting the wood, and getting the wood into the house. Both of these problems involved going out into the freezing abyss that is Wisconsin winter.

My young self did not appreciate the genius move on my parents' part: bribery. "Are you boys ready for hot chocolate and cookies?" my mother would call, noting to herself the woodbin was low. Excitedly, we would head outside, split wood, freeze off a finger and then toss the wood in through a hole in the side of the house.

Ty and I were always excited to come in to hot chocolate and cookies. The odd thing is I don't ever recalling my parents coming outside and helping us. Seems like they were just content watching us from the comfort inside. I guess somebody had to catch the wood and swing the wood door hole closed. Might as well be them.

Ty (right) and me with our Easter baskets

One winter, we were bored, so Ty and I went for a walk down to the lake. The funny thing about Buffalo Lake, the lake near our house, is that it wasn't actually a lake at all. In fact, it was a dammed river. For those new to river or lake living, this means there are a couple problems. First of all, it fills full of weeds in the summer. I'm not talking about the weeds that hit your feet when you swim in it. I'm talking about weeds that hide the Loch Ness Monster. Buffalo "Lake" had three full-time weed eaters who tried to keep some semblance of order for the folks like us who owned a fishing boat.

The second issue is in winter, the water never freezes all the way across. To my parents' credit, especially my father, he always – repeat with me, ALWAYS – told us to stay off the ice.

This day was no different. While putting on our very 1980s stylish ultra-insulated moon boots and snow pants, my dad yelled as we ran out the door, "Boys have fun! But stay off the ice!"

So what did we do? We went out on the ice!

As we walked out, we could see a clearing in the ice. It was our first time we could actually see the water clear. It was like scuba diving! No weeds, perfectly clear. "Ty, come look at this!" I beckoned.

And then, splash.

My brother had fallen through a thin part of the ice and into the water. He was instantly in a current of deep, cold water. By several fortunate acts of God, he is still alive today. Turns out those moon boots and layers of clothing are naturally buoyant. Ty was never fully submerged, and with two hands he was able to grab a thicker part of the ice. Equally fortunate was the fact I was able to pull him out without joining him in an icy bath. I never understood why we were supposed to stay off the ice, but all of a sudden my ten-year-old brain got it and was terrified.

We ran as fast as Ty's waterlogged moon boots would carry us to the house. When we got there, you would have thought my dad had seen a ghost.

"Boys, what happened?"

"Ty fell though the ice."

We were terrified he was going to spank us and lock us into a closet until we were 35. We braced for the onslaught.

"Oh my God, I am so happy you are safe! Don't you ever, EVER go back out on that ice! Never again! Promise?"

I had never seen this man, whom I idolized, so shaken in his entire life. I understood clearly then what we meant to him and how we were bonded as a family. My brother and I would fight for years off and on after that. Yet the thought of him drowning under that ice is a thought to this day that haunts me.

Finally, when a principal's job came up in the Milwaukee suburb of Wauwatosa, my father jumped on the application. Again, out of a deep and experienced pool of applicants, the gentle giant rose to the top. Dad's dream of living near the big city had come to fruition. On top of it all, the new job had a raise in salary and the hours that would need to be spent at the dreaded late-night board meetings were minimized because it was an associate principal position. The downside to the position at Wauwatosa West was it came with the job of disciplining students. Ty and I had grown up with discipline, but there was always a clear reason spelled out for that discipline. This same purposeful style of demonstrating right or wrong with leniency and love was something my father also brought to work with him.

To this day, thanks to the advent of social media, I still hear stories from former students of how meaningful it was to be sent to "Mr. Breitlow's office." I am certain that he felt that same "this is harder on me than it is on you" attitude when suspending someone for wearing a hat to school. Although he never said it to students, his leniency and purposeful words and actions left an imprint that has forever changed the landscape for thousands.

Hindsight being 20/20, there were red flags all over the field that should have alerted us to this new place not being where God wanted us to be. But we pushed on.

For starters, the house in Montello had not sold despite us starting school two hours away. The only problem with the house was its magnificence. It was a beautiful, rustic log cabin style with epic vaulted ceilings and character that can only be found in the craftsmanship of custom-built homes.

There was that infamous wood-burning stove that kept us toasty though the frigid winters and amplified all our Christmas experiences. On top of that, the house came complete with a vast supply of fort-building woodland acreage, access to an incredible – if not thin-iced – fishing lake, and, oh yeah, have I mentioned the pool yet? Living there was the best years of our lives and memories with my family I cherish deeply to this day.

We purchased the house from the outgoing principal and didn't give a thought to an exit strategy. Big oops. This gave us the distinction of the biggest house in town, essentially a mansion. Not a good thing in a town where the average income was a third of the state average.

I recall my mom and dad hiring and firing different real estate agents to sell the house, and they all said the same thing: "To sell this house in this town, you have to lower your price."

The unintended side effects were we lived in Montello on the weekends, and during the week we would live in a cheap hotel near the school. It was almost the exact same thing we had done four years ago.

The good part about this plan was it allowed us to start and finish the school year in the same place with the same friends. The bad news is we were a family of four living in hotels two hours from a house we couldn't afford. Our parents astutely realized that the family was not in a place that lent itself to growth. The short-term solution, which became a three-year disaster, was that we moved an entire woodland house into a small, very cramped apartment.

Given the options of hotel living with a weekly rate versus an apartment, the move made sense. This turned out to be the start of the end for our family.

What were once weekends building forts in the woods and fishing became Ty and I playing video games and watching HBO until we fell asleep. The magic my parents had for us seemed to be fading.

Mercifully, the Montello house sold, and Mom and Dad started looking for a real house in Wauwatosa to resume what we had known as "normal family life." Here more red flags started showing up, which again should have been a sign from God to start moving on to the next place.

Now weekends were spent in a car with an agent wearing way too much perfume, driving around looking at house after house after house. None of them were good enough from where we once lived. So apartment living across the street from a giant Briggs & Stratton assembly plant continued.

By the time my freshman year of high school initiated in 1993, we had been "living" in Wauwatosa for three years. I use the term "living" loosely, because our family's quality of life had decreased so dramatically. The most odd thing about our move to the big city was that the transition was so uncomfortable; again, another sign from the universe that we didn't heed.

In late spring of 1992, exhausted and tired of having ninety percent of our possessions in storage, our parents purchased a nice-sized house with a big lot close to the high school in which I was about to enroll and Dad was the principal Wauwatosa West.

My entire middle school was spent not playing the woods building forts, but in a cramped, 800-square foot apartment. The three years of what felt like jail was over. The icing on the cake was I had just finished the most uncomfortable age of being a human, living through the fog, hormones and hair known as middle school. I was about to go to high school.

Chapter 2

My Pivotal Year – 1993

I was just another high school freshman, the first guy off the bench on the freshman boys' basketball team and social in my group of friends. I had a long-term, pretty girlfriend who, like myself, was learning and exploring the vast open spaces of the opposite sex. I had good grades, though not great. And like everyone else, I was subject to the stresses of peers, homework and teachers. There was this one other thing, however. I was also the principal's son. Well, the associate principal's son.

I started out high school and the long four years as the "principal's son" rather uneventfully. Truth be told, in my heart I was terrified to be the principal's son. Yet the worst thing that happened in the first four months of high school was when I was asked to take down a *Sports Illustrated* Swimsuit Edition photo of Cindy Crawford that was, proudly pinned in my school locker. I guess when you are 16 years young and full of testosterone, you don't necessarily care what other female teachers in the hall think of the lady wearing only a fishnet. Oops.

To this day, I can't tell you for certain whether Dale Breitlow ever knew about my mostly naked, testosterone-producing poster. However, I am certain that if he knew, he smiled and asked his coworker to gently remind me that such paraphernalia is frowned upon in the conservative, suburban public school system.

It was hard to miss Dad in school. At six feet, three inches, three hundred pounds, he was a giant among the pubescent adolescents and teachers alike. It wasn't that my father was obese, but to set the record straight, he was indeed overweight. His diet wasn't great. My brother and I still talk about the late-night cravings the man had for Mrs. Grass' famous chicken noodle soup. Mrs. Grass' soup had this "magic egg" that magically dissolved in the soup. The golden egg had who-knows-what inside, but who cares? It tasted delicious!

Dad was an athletic overweight. He played basketball in high school, and baseball and football at the collegiate level. His passion was football – oh, how he loved football. Decades past his prime, when he roamed the halls, he looked like he could still take a handoff from the quarterback and with his thick fullback-esque frame, slam up the middle with the best of 'em.

That being said, I'd never seen my father stick to a regular exercise routine or go for a run before school. It just wasn't his thing — teaching was. He taught because he believed in not only youth and the public education system, but in all humans.

I was a little afraid of being judged as a goodie-two-shoes-principal's-son by my peers. Okay, I was a lot afraid. But what I didn't truly understand at the time was how well-respected my father was by students and teachers alike. He was respected because teaching was his passion and he wore it on his sleeves.

Simon Sinek, in his brilliant book, *Start With Why*, best sums up my father's role as an educator: "People don't buy what you do; they buy why you do it. And what you do simply proves what you believe."

My mother used to get so frustrated with my father for remembering everything and having an uncanny ability to see all sides of any given situation. I can still hear her saying to me, "It's that photographic memory of his. He sees and remembers *everything*."

It was true. The man was a camera, always rolling and always running back old film, never forgetting, always learning. And laughing. Oh, how my father would laugh.

Have you ever heard laughter from someone you knew was just happy? I'm talking a certain kind of happy, an all-the-time happy. It's an infectious laughter coming from deep in the belly of a man who doesn't care who's watching. Not because others don't matter, but because he was acting from within and without judgment. People loved his authenticity, and this is why people would love and laugh with him.

My brother is gifted with a similar memory and sense of humor. As of today, Ty has taken a similar career path to my father and a strikingly similar "why." At the young age of 30, he rose to his first principal job. I can't imagine the courage my brother has to walk my father's steps every day of his life. Not only does he do it, he also does it with excellence.

I imagine that many teachers at a public high school would have a difficult time answering to a 30-something principal. It takes a certain someone with a certain set of skills to command that respect. Like my father, I believe the trump card for my brother is his organic and authentic passion for people. His love for education and treating others as equals is what sets him apart. I know he learned this modeling from our father.

For now, back to 1993. I was not gifted with the ability to gab or tell jokes. Heck, I still need to write jokes down to remember them! Instead, I was gifted with the natural ability to feel and empathize with others. When you put an empathizer and a great expresser together, the bond they form will surpass any uranium nuclear bonds in the world. That was us, the nuclear bonded father-son.

I can recall many a night having to get up to use the bathroom as a young boy, and without fail, I would see a reflection in the living room signifying the TV was on. There would be my father, on the floor, eating Mrs. Grass' magic egg soup, in tighty-whitey Hanes underwear. Oh, and of course, a matching loose-fitting XXL V-neck white Hanes t-shirt.

These shirts were heaven to me. His belly used to hang out just below the bottom of the shirt, and my shame-free father would walk around, leaving open a huge opportunity for my younger brother and I to "belly fart" him. That time-honored tradition of taking your mouth to another human's stomach area, blowing as hard as you can and reaping the joy of the uncannily similar sound to flatulence. He loved it.

Nine times out of ten when I got up, he was there. Yet he was not there with a bag of chips just watching TV. Nope, the man would vacillate between the sports page of the Milwaukee Journal and whatever new project the Wauwatosa School Board had him working on.

The family room floor, the newspapers and work papers represented my father and all his core values in a nutshell: sports, teaching, and of course, family. To this day, despite being married with a child, I half expect to walk out of bed to use the bathroom and see the TV on down the hall, my underwear-totin' father in prime form. It's why I leave a light on in our living room all night to this day.

What I'm attempting to do here is paint the picture of a family man, one who loved to be alive. He made people feel better about themselves and who they were just by being around them. Here was a supremely talented man who looked at the big picture, knew all angles from any perspective, never using his mind or wit to his advantage. His largest gift was his ability to make friends. He was the Gandhi of Wauwatosa, and nearly everybody saw that. The one person who didn't was Leonard McDowell.

~

Wednesday, December 1, 1993: I was nearing the end of my first semester as a high school freshman. Christmas vacation was within reach, and it was one of those chilly early Midwest winter days where the high and the low temperatures are nearly the same. The skies were grey and overcast, setting the damp, cold mood for the day and many subsequent ones to follow.

I was in Mr. Norstrem's end-of-the-day, sixth-period English class, daydreaming more about basketball practice than Jane Austen, when I heard a siren outside the window. As we didn't live in an urban area, sirens were fairly uncommon but did happen from time-to-time. In the past, I would think, "I wonder where that siren is going." I would picture a fireman rescuing a cat or a cop pulling over a person who rolled through a stop sign.

In that instant, I had one of the most bizarre and random thoughts to ever run through my brain. I specifically remember feeling as if someone had entered my thoughts and planted an unfathomable idea. It was as if God knew exactly what I needed to hear before I actually heard it.

Unconsciously, and almost instantly after I heard the siren, I heard myself think, "Your father has been shot. That siren is here for your father." Returning a moment later to reality, I shook my head and reassuringly convinced myself such a thought was ludicrous.

Of the millions of things that siren could have been, why on earth would it have anything to do with violence at school or with you or your family? The weird thing was, my brain was unable to convince my heart that indeed the illogical thing was also the truth.

About fifteen minutes later, an announcement came across alerting all teachers that when the sixth-period bell rang, we were to remain in our classrooms until further notice. It was actually a secret lockdown code: "Mr. Locker, please report to the office."

The voice in the back of my head said nothing, nor did my brain. I swallowed hard. Real hard. The silence was like God saying, "See, I told you so." My heart began racing. It was racing away to some finish line that didn't exist in a race I never started running. The class was becoming uncomfortable, especially as my mind raced through hundreds of possible explanations and emotions. Another siren, then another, and as Mr. Norstrem was waxing eloquently about "Pride and Prejudice," I just wanted to look out the window. Thank God I never did.

Then came a knock on the classroom door. It was one of the school's guidance counselors. He quietly asked to speak to me, suggesting I grab my books and come with him.

Panic. Internal panic. God in my brain, sitting up there saying, "I told you so."

We slowly walked down the hall into an empty conference room. Before Mr. Marten could get the words out of his mouth, that voice, that damn voice told me again, "Jay, your father's been shot". I imagine that Mr. Marten was not prepared for the perplexed look on my face, because thank God — thank the beautiful God for whatever unknown things were happening to me – a sixth sense gave my soul a "knowing" that something was wrong.

As he told me what happened, or at least as much as he knew, my life came crashing down all around. Literally, everything I had every known changed in that instant. But because a connection to God or the universe or whatever stepped in and told me before a human did, the grief was considerably more tolerable. To continue without being despondent or hysterical was no minor miracle for me.

A fifteen-minute ride to the hospital ensued. By the time we arrived, scores of reporters and cameras already were waiting to greet us. Amazing to think that prior to cellphones and smartphones, news, especially tragic news, traveled so quickly.

We were led to the waiting room; this small, albeit cozy, waiting area where countless people before and after us had no doubt endured similar feelings of hope and hopelessness. I remember just sitting there, already knowing in my heart of hearts what had happened. My brain was now believing God and my soul. I sat in a very 1980s style couch, wondering what happens next, and how they tell people like us that life as they knew it is over.

Then it happened. It was just an instant, a half-second where the waiting room door opened to let someone out to head to the restroom. I saw a man walking down the hallway. I heard God tell me again, in that voice, "He's here to tell you that he didn't make it. He's the one."

Sure enough, the doctor, clearly in new scrubs he just changed into, told us, "Ma'am I'm sorry. We did all we could, but we couldn't save your husband."

Absolute chaos.

My mother broke out in tears. My brother cried with a neighbor while some random person grabbed and hugged me. Mom was inconsolable, distraught. Ty was the same. I stared straight ahead, tearless. Who were all these people?

The first thing my mother said when she could finally talk was, "I have to call Vi and Elmer. They can't hear this on the news first."

Vi and Elmer Breitlow, my father's parents and longtime farmers, had literally just retired. They had sold decades of work on the farm for a house closer to family in a town of three thousand. They had just moved in and no doubt were still getting used to their surroundings.

My father's love for life he no doubt inherited from his parents, especially my grandfather. Grandpa Elmer was the man. He was known as a kind and gentle guy who said little, but when he spoke, it was always powerful and on purpose. Both he and my father would laugh together, one quiet and grinning; the other belly-deep and open-mouthed. They were wonderful together.

One of my favorite memories of childhood is of my father and Grandpa Elmer on the lake in an inflatable boat. The boat was designed to fit two teenage children, not two adults. But here on vacation at the lake, were all 250-plus pounds of Dad and 150 pounds of Grandpa stuffed into a nearly sinking rowboat. Neither swam well, and both wore life vests that didn't fit. They each had a beer in hand and were having the times of their lives. These child-like scenes seemed to happen all the time with these two young-at-hearts. I miss them both deeply to this day.

My Grandpa Elmer

After December 1, 1993, that radiant smile Elmer had shown the world was never seen again. With the loss of my father, Christmases would never be the same. That year's Christmas, only days removed from the funeral, was especially sad.

In the spirit of tradition, we still got together as an extended family, just like we did every year previously. I recall Granny Vi shedding tears now and then after opening a gift. We all cried a bit getting together that year. But this Christmas, just days after his son's death, Grandpa just sat on the couch. He would open a gift here and there, politely thank the giver, and then just sit. That first Christmas, I get it; but one year later as the rest of the family seemingly was moving on, Grandpa was the exact same.

I'm seventeen at this point, and pretty oblivious to what is going on around me unless it involves the opposite sex. But it was obvious Grandpa just wasn't the same. He never was the same. On April 11, 1995, Elmer Breitlow died of what was called a stroke. Call it whatever you want, but Grandpa lost the will to live and wanted to be with his son. I have heard stories of broken hearts, but I had never actually seen it play out in real life. Not until then.

The details of my father's shooting would start to come out over the next couple days and drag on for another year and a half as the trial wrapped up. The man who took my father's life was a former student, Leonard McDowell, and he ultimately received a life sentence in prison for first degree murder.

In the course of the investigation and subsequent trial, officials determined Leonard killed my father for the simple reason he was upset with him.

Dad was the enforcer at school, and as he was the person who called the police to remove him from the school numerous times from 1990-1991, Leonard felt he needed to get even with him. Quoted at the trial, Leonard said he was either going to "kill Mr. Breitlow or kill myself."

According to reports, Leonard was stalking a teacher in a hallway on December 5, 1990. The timeline is unclear to me, but I believe Leonard had either graduated or left school a few months earlier. When he came back to Wauwatosa West months later, he grabbed and attempted to molest his former teacher. The teacher recalled that Leonard "grabbed my head with both hands and kissed my cheek." She later stated that she "wasn't sure if he was going to rape me or choke me."

My father, despite his big, bruising fullback size, called the police first to support and escort Leonard from the building. However, as the teacher had called for help, Leonard fled the building. Yet for some unknown reason, he chose to return a short time later. This is when the police, four grown men, arrested Leonard. Leonard was a thick guy and didn't go easily. In fact, it took the officers twenty minutes to cuff and remove him from school.

This was the event that changed the course of Leonard's life – and my own. After his removal and subsequent arrest, he was released from jail and signed into a mental health institution. He was treated for an unspecified number of days, but based on similar cases, I deduce he was incarcerated no more than a week.

Subsequent events would involve Leonard with local police, as well as his former teacher at Wauwatosa West. One day, he broke into the school intoxicated, found his way into the pool and was discovered by police swimming in his underwear. On another occasion, he was found drunk in the neighborhood, hanging out under a bridge overpass.

This type of non-violent behavior was a more regular event, as was the police coming to the family home when they or a neighbor called the police because Leonard became drunk and unruly. He was also found wandering into the high school to get food from a vending machine long after he was out of school.

Leonard continued to stalk the former teacher at her house about a year after the school-kissing event. When police arrested him again, he couldn't (or didn't) pay the fine and lost his driver's license. The realization came to me as I was writing this book that this one single event likely saved my life.

After Leonard was arrested for shooting my father, police found damning evidence against him in the form of handwritten notes. The notes included his plans to kill my father. They contained my father's name and shorthand details to himself about how he was going to come to our residence and do it.

Following Leonard's arrest at the school in 1990, he received a copy of his violation. Protocol at the time required the person who made the call to the police to have their name and address listed as the prosecution. This is exactly how Leonard was able to obtain our address, straight down to the apartment number.

Due to this specific event, schools across the country now use the school's address rather than an individual staff member, with all information related to the teachers and administration remaining private.

The challenge for Leonard was by the time he decided to extract his revenge, we had moved. All he had was our old address. Leonard didn't know we had moved, and when he came to the apartment, he saw somebody else and plotted to find Dad another way.

Since the high school was directly across the street from his house, Leonard chose this as a far easier confrontation location than finding our current residence. To this day, I have a difficult time wrapping my head around how nobody else got hurt. Fortunately, nobody did.

Moments before the shooting happened, a neighbor recalled seeing Leonard go for one of his routine walks from his house to check the mailbox and continue on his way toward the school.

This day, as the neighbor was hanging Christmas lights, he reported seeing Leonard stop at the mailbox, but instead of opening and looking, he paused for a moment before continuing on his route. I wonder what was going through his mind. Was he having second thoughts? Like so many of you reading this book, I often wonder, "What was he thinking?" anytime I hear of violence on TV, especially in a school setting.

Around 2 p.m. on December 1, students in calculus class reported hearing my father and Leonard in the hallway. "What are you doing here? What are you doing here?" they heard my father say. The answer came with three gunshots, one to the leg, one to the abdomen, and the fatal shot to his heart.

Students recalled seeing my father fall to the floor after the first shot, at which point two girls ran for help and the reminder of the class was moved away from the windows. I remember thinking in court months later that my dad would have survived the first two shots, but nobody lives with a broken heart. It was true for a giant, loving man like my dad against a bullet, as well as the ripple effect on my grandpa eighteen months later.

Classmates thought of Leonard as a bit odd, but nobody really thought he was a physical threat to himself or anybody else. A classmate recalled in 1993 in the *Milwaukee Journal*: "When he talked, he didn't always make sense. From what I remember, he would say things and for a while he made sense, but then you couldn't understand what he was talking about."

Another student stated in the paper: "I always thought he just wanted attention. I can just picture him making (this) facial expression." The expression was one in which he would smile and shake his head furiously.

His neighbors told a slightly more disturbing story. As one neighbor recalled, "He never talked to me, never said hello. The police were always [at the house]. They had a hard time getting him out sometimes. We knew something was wrong with him. It's sad he never got helped."

Leonard ultimately was deemed fit for trial despite some healthcare professionals giving mental diagnoses that included schizophrenia, Tourette syndrome, paranoia and anxiety. In some reports, Leonard admitted to the shooting; in others, he claimed innocence. He still filed a not guilty claim, but with the dozens of eye witnesses, the gun at his house and notes in his house detailing his plan to "Kill Mr. Breitlow," the case was fairly open and shut.

As of the writing of this book, Leonard is still serving out his life sentence at a correctional facility in Central Wisconsin. Very little has been heard of him, although four years later he unsuccessfully appealed the court decision.

Sources

"McDowell mentally fit for murder trial," by David Doege, Jan. 14, 1994, *Milwaukee Sentinel*, page 5A.

"Suspect talked about buying a gun, former co-worker says," by McCoy, et al; Dec. 3, 1993, *Milwaukee Journal*, page 1B.

Chapter 3

Healing

There is no "one-size-fits-all" recipe for dealing with the loss of a loved one, and certainly not for children who lose a parent. What happened to me is what I suspect happens to most children who tragically lose a parent: your lifelong mentor is gone in a flash. Or even worse, for children who tragically lose two parents, both your mentors are gone. As challenging as it has been for me to move forward with my life, I can't even imagine losing both parents.

After the loss of my mentor, my mother played a bigger role in my life, and I know loves me more now than ever. She mentored me with many things, but one event in particular sticks out. When I was a college freshman, I made up my mind that I was going to be on the crew team. I had never been part of a rowing team at any point in my life, and frankly, I was just an average high school athlete. But I had an older friend from high school who was on a crew team in college and encouraged me to see if Purdue had a team when I got there.

Lo and behold, I called the coach when I got to campus, and when the team had an informal meeting, I was in the first row. I had spent the entire summer lifting weights at our local YMCA, and for the first time in my life was beginning to care how my body would move when pushed toward its limits.

Sweet! When do I get started? Conveniently, two weeks into practice and involved hook, line and sinker, I learned there was a dues schedule that needed attention. Since the Purdue crew team was a club sport and not a scholarship program like the swim team or basketball teams, everybody had to pay their way. The tab for the entire year? Two thousand bucks!

I was devastated. I was already going to an out-of-state program (read: more than double the tuition of an in-state Wisconsin school) and felt so guilty for taking so much of my mom's resources to go to school. Looking at the "future tab" just to have the pleasure of rowing, and subsequently puking my brains out from the toll of competition, I couldn't see how it was going to happen.

I told the coach I would call my mom and see what we as a family could do. The coaches were uber-supportive and they thought my role on the team was going to be vital for years to come. So I called my mom, told her about the first two weeks of practice, and then dropped the bomb.

Expecting my mom to give a "Well, at least you had a great first couple practices," and then talk about the importance of studies and my future, she had a totally different response. Instead, she hit back with "Two thousand bucks?"

"Yep, two grand, Mom."

"Honey, in the grand scheme of things, two thousand bucks is nothing."

After I picked my mouth up off the floor, I stammered some response like, "What? You heard me say two grand, right?"

"Jay, if this is something you really want to do and something you will enjoy, the money is nothing. If you need it and things get tight, I'll help you out."

I was overjoyed. I had gone from ecstasy over the discovery of a new sport I was actually good at, straight to the doldrums over the prospect of not competing, and right back to above and beyond ecstasy. It was a side of my mother I had rarely seen. Certainly, one I had not seen much of the last four years. I knew my mother loved me, which was never a question, but to feel that love over the phone, without hesitation or reservation, was a feeling I will always hold onto.

Many of my best friends and certainly the best experiences of my collegiate life came out of the crew team. I still keep in touch with many of the guys and some of the girls on the team to this day. I have shared holidays, been groomsmen in some of their weddings, and have enjoyed seeing many of their children come into the world.

When my mom encouraged me to forget about the money and just work at being the best oarsmen I could be, it was one of the best decisions I, ever made. I reminded her of that experience recently, and she had no recollection of it. What this tells me is it was truly a decision that was a part of her. She couldn't separate herself into a money side and a love side.

She only had the love for her child, and so it came with a $2,000 price tag. So what? Thank you, Mom! Thank you for strengthening our family through the most challenging of family dynamics that I can imagine. Thank you for keeping me sane and guiding me to a decision that offered balance in my life.

~

Dr. Wayne Dyer is an internationally renowned author and speaker in the field of self-development. He has written forty-plus books in his lifetime, all of which have dramatically changed the lives of millions of people around the world. In nearly every book, he has referenced love as the answer to violence. He has a well-titled book, *There's a Spiritual Solution to Every Problem,* and – I state for the record – I am going to steal that line and note that this very book could easily be titled "There's a Loving Solution for Every Act of Violence."

The great thing about his writing is he talks to people in common-sense terms. In fact, his first book, *Your Erroneous Zones,* was written almost to spite the technical research, "APA-style" community. At one point in his career at St. Johns College in New York, he came to a crossroads: write technical papers with a litany of references or talk to people in terms that are easily understood.

I really developed an appreciation for Dr. Dyer's writing when I stumbled upon a paper written by a couple of PhDs that attempted to scientifically figure out what children are to do when they lose a parent. It's an extremely detailed and fully cited scientific paper entitled "Evidence-Based Practices for Parentally Bereaved Children and Their Families." In an attempt to cover all my bases and understand as much as I can about how other children in my shoes see the world, I opened this article and promptly fell asleep.

The aforementioned paper does have its merits, and in between naps, one of the more simply worded phrases, and perhaps the "duh" moment of the day, found its way to me: "The death of a parent during childhood is a traumatic event that places children at risk for several negative outcomes."

The paper goes on to talk about potential "solutions" for the loss of the parent and how to avoid "negative outcomes."

"Negative outcome" is an interesting phrase, and one that got me thinking about life in general. I wanted to find out how many Americans are "happy." My thought process is this: if you aren't happy in life, that – to me – is a negative outcome. Period. If you are happy, that's a positive outcome.

I know the study defined the outcomes differently, but if we are honest, isn't that what we all want? Happiness? According to a 2010 Gallup poll, 40 percent of Americans say they are struggling or trying to be happy.

Walking down the street, that means almost half the people you walk past are unhappy or seeking to find happiness. I look at somebody like Wayne Dyer, and when I see and hear him talk, I almost always am happier. I picture a happy man with a happy family. Yet, in reality, here is a man who openly talks about how he has experienced loss, sadness, depression, divorce and a litany of other life challenges.

When I read about a man of his stature who has gone through challenges and has been "unhappy," it gives me hope; not only for my life, but for the lives of everyone in the world. The details of his life experiences and the challenges he has faced are discussed wonderfully in his book *I Can See Clearly Now*. If the Gallup poll had come around and asked me if I was happy, I would almost always place myself in the "happy" category. Yet there are times that I, like Wayne Dyer, would have answered no.

Give yourself permission to be unhappy sometimes. Loss happens in life. It is, in fact, inevitable. The phrase "Tis better to have loved and lost, then to have never loved at all" is 100 percent valid. Be it loss of money, property, family, career, friends or health, there will come a day for change. The question is: how will you deal with loss?

The scientific snoozers, along with nearly everything I have read and experienced in life, lead me to the same conclusion: it is necessary in life to have mentorship. Without a mentor, you are missing guidance, partnership, support, love and friendship, among other things both tangible and intangible.

Fortunately for me, since that tragic and grey December day in 1993, I have had two people support me personally, unwaveringly and beyond the means of ordinary humans. I will talk about them soon, yet calling attention to these two in no way minimizes the incredible support I have received from literally thousands of other people.

We have a close-knit family, both maternal and paternal. They all were instrumental in helping me thrive. My classmates at every institution I have attended, including Wauwatosa West, Purdue University and Palmer College of Chiropractic Medicine, all gave a thirst to my soul to be somebody. The communities I have lived in have all been amazing. Longmont, Colorado, has taken us in and nurtured me to write this book.

Yet thinking about Wauwatosa still makes me emotional. There were candlelight vigils and memorials attended by the thousands. There were green ribbons tied around trees and worn on lapels in support for months at a time. West had a five-foot-tall graffiti rock that was spray-painted and not touched in memorial for nearly a year. We received – and I am not exaggerating – thousands of letters, cards, notes, prayer chains and gifts. The Wauwatosa School District dedicated a sports field, something my father would have LOVED, as "Breitlow Field."

I can't imagine who and what I am forgetting here, but you get the idea. We were loved, and that has made a huge difference in my life. I did go back to walking the halls at West. I walked past, and probably over, the spot where my father took his last breath. That I didn't go off the deep end and experience a "negative outcome," I can only thank the thousands of named and unnamed in the Wauwatosa community.

A unique thing still happens to this day through the magic of social media. Every December 1st, whether I remember to post a note on Facebook in memorandum or not, I receive hundreds of mini "thinking of you" notes. I state this here again to note just how wonderful people are and how moving a human my dad was.

With any event, both good and bad, there comes a point when people return back to their own lives. It's human nature. The process of having many people support you immediately is vital, in my experience. But two years later when you need somebody to guide you through choosing a college or dating a pretty girl or rooting for the Packers—who do you do those things with? Especially when the person who, in your mind, was supposed to be there for forever and ever, amen, is gone?

The support I received in 1993 was and still is astounding, and has largely kept me from myself, so to speak. But without individual mentorship, I likely would have been and still be lost. My two individual mentors are my Uncle Gary, whom I have known my whole life, and my life and business coach, Dr. Tom Preston, whom I met in 2008. Since I met Tom later in life, he comes later in my story, but Gary is someone who stepped up on December 1, 1993, and is still by my side today.

Gary was one of my mom's eleven siblings and the only one who wasn't married at the time of my father's death. He didn't have kids and lived in nearby Chicago, making growth easy between us, both in high school (ninety minutes from Wauwatosa) and in college (Purdue was another short ninety-minute drive).

When we weren't together on the weekends, we would talk on the phone for hours at a time. We were two bachelors who loved the same stuff. We would often end up talking about sports, dating and career opportunities. He was climbing the ladder on Chicago's LaSalle Street financial district, and I was climbing the collegiate and business rungs.

The trivialities of how often and what we talked about aren't important to this book. What is important is I had somebody to fill a huge void in my life as a mentor. I had another male who could be there for me while celebrating on New Year's Eve or licking my wounds the morning after.

I remember one weekend in particular when I was at Purdue. It must have been sometime in late 1999 and I was likely a junior. I had been very involved with a girl at the time and was certain I was in love. Then I caught her cheating on me. It was the first time I had experienced a relationship break off like that. I was angry, distraught, disappointed, emotionally empty and heartbroken all at the same time.

So what did I do? I immediately went back to my apartment, burned all her pictures, packed my bags and drove the ninety minutes to Chicago. Gary and I proceeded to have a wonderful heart-to-heart over lunch downtown, and he took the rest of the day off to hang out. We went for a jog, then out to dinner, just two guys out on the town.

I wasn't a very big drinker in college, but I would go to a party every other weekend and drink a bit too much every now and then. After dinner, Gary and I ended up in an upscale part of Chicago known as Rush Street. We had gone out down here on prior occasions, but never to the smaller, less-upscale bar called Bootleggers. Gary recalls how I was drowning my sorrows by playing kissy-face at the bar with a young grade school teacher while he babysat me. I guess the best way to get over a breakup is to get right back on the horse.

Nights like Bootleggers were a rare exception. Normally we would kick it in Chicago and go to dinner or waltz around downtown. Sometimes Gary would take me skiing in Colorado to the mountain town of Vail. Vail, to this day, is my favorite ski resort, and I am positive it was our trips together westward which led me ultimately to live here.

This is what mentors do. This is how voids are filled in people lives – with love! I had my life and my sanity because of Gary's fatherly, brotherly, "uncley" and fraternal love. I didn't just survive the college years – I thrived. At a time where my development could have gone so awry, I actually turned into an okay dude.

My life after college zigzagged. I went straight to a very unfulfilling career as a nuclear engineer in Virginia. I just didn't like the work and ended up quitting. In fact, I may go down in history as one of the worst engineers of all time. I proceed to spend my hard-saved 401(k) on a year traveling the South Pacific. Unable to find a future in the world as a vagabond loner, I decided a career as a chiropractor would be an excellent fit. So my next stop was the oldest and most renowned chiropractic school in the world. The problem was Palmer College was in Iowa.

I actually loved my three-year "career" as a chiropractic student in Iowa. When I wasn't in school, you could find me dabbling in the world of triathlons. It was during this time that I competed – and did quite well – finishing multiple Ironman-length triathlons. After graduation, I took a short maternity coverage stint at a chiropractic office in Nebraska. This allowed me to save up some coin before I moved to Africa.

I made the move to Ghana in West Africa, in early 2009. My grand plan was a noble one, just one that in the end didn't suit me. I had started a non-profit company called Journey to Solidarity with the idea that I could combine two of my most favorite things in life: chiropractic and traveling. The goal was to help as many people as possible, and chiropractic was my vehicle.

One of the things that may be new to you is that chiropractic does so much more than just improve lives by getting rid of headaches, neck pains or lower back issues. What I wanted to tell people in Africa is exactly what I tell people in my practice in Colorado today: that by removing nervous system interference, you allow your body and all its systems to function at a higher level.

My vision was to spend years collecting data about the relationship between the benefits of chiropractic care and people afflicted with HIV/AIDS. My hypothesis was that as patients are given a chiropractic adjustment, their neuro/immune response would improve to the point where their body would fight the disease more effectively by itself. There are some magnificent studies out there looking at the improvements in visceral body functions with chiropractic. I wanted to do one also.

The problem was twofold. I really was never cut out to do research or write technical papers. I always knew there was the possibility for huge life improvements with chiropractic, both subjectively and objectively. However, when I began to see that for myself in patients, it somehow seemed to make the research side of life less important. My second problem? I met a girl.

I first met Christina when I was walking around Accra, the capital city of Ghana, on a sweltering Sunday afternoon. She was wondering why on earth anybody would be walking around this city sight-seeing and not staying cool inside. Frankly, she thought I was crazy and didn't want anything to do with me, at least romantically speaking.

As we were both doing some work for a man who owned two local clinics, it was inevitable that we would meet. Christina was working in a 100 percent for-profit environment and had wonderful experiences, just as I did working in a partial for-profit/non-profit clinic.

In the end, the man who brought us over individually saw us leave together. Unfortunately, it was not the most nurturing environment for us individually or as a team. Sometimes, learning how you don't want to treat people is as important as learning how you would like to treat people, especially those with whom you work.

Eventually, we decided we wanted to start a family back in the states. Christina and I both got jobs working in the same office in the suburbs of Chicago. This situation, ironically, wasn't that different from the one we left in Africa: working for somebody who didn't fully embrace who we were as individuals. This was going to drive us crazy. We were never going to grow as individuals.

On top of that, even if the work environment was 100 percent awesome, neither of us wanted to work for somebody the rest of our lives. We wanted to be entrepreneurs.

In early 2010, we started looking at business plans and what our own office would look like in our ideal world. We tried for months to start a clinic in a nearby suburb, but ultimately in 2010, just a year and a half from the start of the great recession, we were unable to get a loan.

Enter my next mentor, Dr. Tom Preston. Dr. Tom is a chiropractor turned life and business coach in Ontario, Canada. Christina and I credit Tom with saving our marriage, as I alluded to earlier. Prior to that, Tom gave us the tools we needed to start our own chiropractic practice in Colorado.

Included in our fees were detailed financial spreadsheets, planning tools, marketing ideas and expected hurdles to clear. Our inability to get a $150,000 startup loan turned into a blessing, as he instead showed how a $25,000 equipment loan in a different setting would do even more for us.

What was not expected as part of the process is what's of most interest to this book. Dr. Tom, or simply Coach, had me look into the tragedy of my father's "early life transition." (That's coach speak for "tragic death.") He was concerned the negatives of this experience would loom and potentially destroy me if I was unable to see the positives. The kneejerk reaction was, "Yeah right, there is nothing positive about this."

Yet Coach asserted that there were and continues to be positives from this experience. Are there enough positives that I would ever sit back someday and say, "Boy, my life is better without my father?" Absolutely not!

However, what he wanted me to do was shift away from being the victim. Shift away from somebody stuck in a rut, pissed-off that life dealt him a shit hand. He encouraged me to start looking and living through the positive experiences of the past and recreate those in the future for my family and myself. So I had a homework assignment: Write a list of positives that came from Dad's physical death.

Note the key word here is "physical." I know that my father is still with me to this day and always will be. He lives on in the memories of his students, his family, his DNA in his children and grandchildren, and of course, his eternal spirit. I feel his love and joy in so many things I do – and don't do, for that matter. Every time I have a difficult decision, if I sit still long enough, I feel his presence in the room, guiding me to choose the most authentic decision.

Millions of people around the world, in addition to research done at Harvard University, have documented the importance of silence. I had dabbled in silence, specifically meditation, for the previous year of my life.

Whenever we would lose power in Ghana, the normal routine would be to light a candle and wait the ten minutes to an hour for the lights to come back on. One particular night, I was eating dinner when the power took a little longer to return. As I was eating solo this night, I had the privilege of a candlelight dinner with my own company.

All of a sudden, I wasn't alone. I felt a stiff breeze and then an eerie, almost calm-before-the-storm type of silence. I was sure it was my dad who was with me.

So I sat there with a candle eating dinner, talking with the darkness and the spirit of my father. It was a transformative dinner. I thanked him for guiding me through the difficult decisions I had made in life: quitting a job I hated, selling my 401k to travel for a year, starting a career that was foreign to me and moving to Africa to follow my heart. Perhaps that is why doing the exercise to link the positive of his death was easier than I imagined at first. It's also why I know he is physically transitioned, but spiritually and eternally with us.

I initially challenged Tom when he asked me to write a list of twenty positives. When that challenge disappeared, I decided to take it to the next level: "I bet I could do 50."

"Yeah, but could you do a 100?" Tom questioned.

"Fine, give me a week. I'll give you a list of 150 positives."

"Done."

By doing this exercise, it allowed me to forgive Leonard for what he did. It didn't absolve him, nor will I ever forget what happened. Forgiveness works because it frees us, not others, from what happens or happened. This exercise freed me from the chains of sadness, depression and darkness that were still in my life. It didn't take away my fear, as I wasn't able to fully let go of it until that day on Tom's dock two years later. But boy, was it a start. It was the start that has led me to share this book with you.

With these chains free, I have been able to go back in time, look at past events and examine them without falling to pieces. I'm still able to balance being a chiropractor (which I love, by the way), a husband, friend, father and writer. I have my mentors to thank for this.

I guess if you watch enough movies or TV, you feel your life playing out like it's on the screen. For at least twenty years, I saw my life in an "after" picture. You know the routine. A mother and daughter lose their husband in a high-profile accident. *60 Minutes* or the news covers the story to talk about what happened and address the question, "Where are they now?"

What it doesn't show you are the grief and loss in-between. All they generally show are current pictures of Mom pushing her daughter happily on the swing. The scene is meant to capture that life goes on and people can experience love again. This is all very, very true. As of recently in my life, I have loved more every day than the previous one.

Yet, this "after" picture of my life had me living in a future where everything was all hunky-dory; some magic place you get to without travelling down the road of reality. I justify this magic wand thought process by saying, "I was protecting myself." Perhaps I was, but it unquestionably kept me from grieving.

I never grieved the loss of the most important person in my world. Life doesn't have any shortcuts, friends. No sir. Ask me how I know. I would grieve later in life in my own unique way, and it would almost ruin my marriage to the most supporting, loving woman I have ever met.

This book is a story about love, a testament to its power and timelessness. This is just the first of many ways I believe love can intervene and change the world for the better. It was the strength and fortitude of love for my wife Christina, and her unconditional, unwavering nature that got us through the worst of times.

Our story is a perfect love story that contains many parallels. Both Christina and I began careers in corporate America that we hated. After four years working for 'the man,' we quit those jobs and moved on to new and exciting second careers. We both began education as chiropractors and started that career path working in Ghana. Of course, it was there that we met!

When Christina and I met in Ghana that hot afternoon, I contend it was love at first sight. She will tell you it was something else, and she very much wanted to avoid the sweaty white guy. But she couldn't keep her eyes – or her hands – off me, I tell ya'! We spent much of our time talking, meditating and bringing the love and joy of our newly found chiropractic profession to the people of West Africa. It was a magical time for us, one we grew into.

You are welcome to believe whatever you want about whether it was love at first sight or a slow crescendo. But one thing for certain is this: When she left Ghana for the final time, she knew that as a strong, independent African-American woman, she went all the way to Africa to bring back a white man.

On top of that, we both lost our fathers long before a child is "supposed to" lose a parent.   We had an awareness that our fathers' transitions early in life created a special bond between us. Two years later, what was once a bond became an open, painful wound. Christina had dealt with the loss of her father when she was much younger, whereas I was still living in the *60 Minutes* after scene. I was ready for the wedding and babies and sunny 72-degree, swing-pushing weather.

Two decades of not grieving ultimately led to me having a growing tide of fear. The fear wasn't so much that Christina was in danger, but a mind-altered reality of her impending death. That "someday she might die" is what drove my fear. The potential for loss drove me to create as many ways as possible to protect her and our relationship.

Try telling a strong woman that you are protecting her and you've got it all under control. Let me know how that works out for ya'. It didn't for me, nor I suspect for any human being. Ever.

I was never possessive of Christina. In fact, I still frequently tell her, "If other guys aren't interested in you, then likely they are blind or gay."

A year after we left Ghana, Christina and I were engaged to be married. Two years later, still engaged, as a couple we were drifting. As individuals, we had decided it was over.

The funny thing was neither of us had told the other the words, "It is over." Yet we both knew. In one last attempted hurrah, we made a trip to Ontario for a couple's retreat with our now mentor, friend and coach, Dr. Tom.

We were both pissed and mad as we drove to his lake lodge. The place is in bumble-nowhere and required us flying from Denver, Colorado, to Buffalo, New York, picking up a four-by-four rental, then driving two hours to Toronto, fighting traffic all the way, then another six hours directly north into seeming nothingness. We were a couple headed for breakup – a messy one, seeing as we were going to be splitting up bank accounts, a six-figure business, cars, retirement accounts. You get the idea.

You could cut the tension with a knife as we were forced to travel together for the better part of two days. At the end of it, I remember looking at Christina and saying verbatim, "This (insert adult vernacular here) retreat better be worth it or I'm outta' here!"

Turns out on a dock of the lake, on the corner of one of the most secluded lots on God's green earth, we figured out that never grieving the loss of my father was preventing me from 100 percent stepping into love. Christina let go of some similar energetic blocks that weekend, although certainly not as epic as mine. Those moments changed our lives and showed us how to love, not just each other, but the world.

Losing your father, best friend, confidant, sports pal, coach, mentor and teacher overnight results in huge "negative outcomes." It drives even the most well-intentioned and loving people to a corner they never dreamed they would be backed into. I am writing this book in the hope that more people experience love and choose to express love in their lives. My hope is that my tragedy serves you as a tool to speak about love.

I had no idea that my "after photo" from December 1, 1993, would take twenty-one years to realize. So many years lost at sea without a compass. On top of that, five of those years were spent with a compass that I had no idea how to read, making the thought even more powerful. Christina is my compass, as most every spouse can be in the context of relationship.

Now that I have a better idea how to read it, life is amazing. Granted, sometimes the hormonal fields of Venus interfere with my ability to read the compass from Mars, but that is for another book at another time. I once heard that your spouse is not the person who likes the exact same things as you. Life with marriage is not about both partners wanting the crusts of their creamy peanut butter and jelly sandwiches cut off and sliced diagonally. Instead, the best marriages are the ones in which you can feel free to show your deepest and darkest sides, and they love you just the same. In fact, I assert that you love each other more because of that depth.

Sources

"Evidence-Based Practices for Parentally Bereaved Children and Their Families," Rachel A. Haine, Ph.D, Tim S. Ayers, Ph.D, Irwin N. Sandler, Ph.D, and Sharlene A. Wolchik, Ph.D. Prof Psychology Res Pr. Author manuscript; available in PMC Jun 21, 2010.

Published in final edited form as:
Prof Psychol Res Pr. Apr 2008; 39(2): 113–121.
DOI: 10.1037/0735-7028.39.2.113
PMCID: PMC2888143
NIHMSID: NIHMS109734

Chapter 4

The Rise of School-Related Violence

Since 1993, school-related violence, both with respect to incident count and most certainly in proportion, is on the rise. Mass shootings are becoming an ever more frightening and common headline.

The event that most people look to as the first headlining tragedy occurred in Colorado in April of 1999 at Columbine High School. Before taking their own lives, eighteen-year-old Eric Harris and his best friend, seventeen-year-old Dylan Klebold, killed twelve students, one teacher, and wounded twenty-one others on a cold spring day.

The violence at Columbine could have been much larger in scale, as the two shooters had actually planned for pipe bombs and gas cylinders to explode as well. Fortunately, these plans failed and lives were spared.

The largest school shooting in U.S. history happened eight years later at Virginia Tech in April, 2007. In two separate attacks within two hours, senior student Seung-Hui Cho shot and killed thirty-two people and wounded another seventeen before he also committed suicide.

Five years later, on December 14, 2012 – nineteen years almost to the date of my father's shooting – Newtown, Connecticut, went through the horror that was the second-largest school massacre in U.S. history. During this horrific attack at Sandy Hook Elementary School, twenty first-grade children, all six- to seven-years-old, were killed. This senseless day also took the lives of four elementary school teachers, the principal and the school psychologist.

The final death toll at Newtown was twenty-eight people. The shooter, Adam Lanza, shot his mother at home prior to going to the school. He killed himself before police could take him into custody.

Suicides at the end of these rampages are obviously quite common, as is the shooting of someone familiar – in this case, Lanza's mother. But oftentimes classmates, a familiar foe, a teacher or a group who "wronged" the shooter are the target.

The shocking part with the Sandy Hook tragedy was the twenty elementary school children who died had no known contact with the shooter. They hadn't conceivably wronged him or created undue stress in his life.

This remains a point of discussion. At six years of age, there is no way these children could protect themselves, run, hide or inflict damage to the shooter. This young adult was driven by something dark, deep and unemotional. It is likely we will never know or fully understand the reason or root cause that led to this massacre. What we can and will discuss eventually is what creates a violent mind and the psychological sides of the shooters. But for now, the focus is on the implement of choice: guns.

Adding to the list of high-profile violent cases, I am also choosing to include the July 2012 mass shooting by James Holmes at a *Batman* movie premiere in Aurora, Colorado. In this shooting, twelve innocent people were killed and an additional seventy more were injured. I include it because, despite this book being largely about school-related violence, the topic traverses all violence. Even if it were only school-related, this event would likely fit the bill, as Mr. Holmes was enrolled as a student at the University of Colorado and just as easily could have recreated a Virginia Tech scene instead of a movie theatre massacre.

All events generated huge, international headlines, unanimously uniting local, national, and world communities to grieve over innocent people. What is lost with each of these high-profile shootings are the myriad of violent gun attacks in between, many of them school-related. Some took life, some not. Yet all these incidents included attempts or threats on life within the confines of a building that should be considered a safe learning or family environment.

This book never was and never will be an endorsement for either side of the gun debate – or the middle of the political spectrum, for that matter. Any bias that comes out is merely accidental and likely interpreted by the reader based on their own political beliefs. It's nearly impossible to read or watch anything and at least in part run your life experiences through it as a filter, thereby creating a subconscious bias.

Try as I might to ignore this topic, to not write this book, to continue on my happy way as a chiropractor, it just wasn't happening. The fact is, even when there is a time lapse between violent events, the topic of what to do with guns keeps appearing. The conversation most often surfaces at an anniversary of one of these events or when there is a new development regarding a trial.

I've seen the most miniscule of news related to one of the four high-profile shootings turned into a headline, and time and again it gives a platform for somebody to express an option of what should be done. And the question always – and I do mean always, not often or frequently– centers on what is being done to further the gun debate.

What is lost in between the high profile shootings like Sandy Hook or Virginia Tech is just how frequent smaller cases are, like my father's. Initially, I thought I could write about each school-related shooting and link them together. However, there are hundreds, if not thousands, of violent events between 1993 and today.

Wikipedia has compiled a list of violent attacks in schools dating back to the 1800s. I know Wikipedia shouldn't be held as gospel, but the sheer magnitude of the list is mind-blowing. Looking at the list, I learned that the most deadly attack actually happened in 1927 when a farmer blew up a school in Bath, Michigan, killing forty-five people – including his wife and later himself.

The list very much lengthens and increases at time goes by. As the dots in between shootings get closer and closer, I can't help but think things have to change.

Without getting into more boring stats and cases, thereby putting you straight to sleep, trust me, violent outbursts in schools are indeed on the rise. Crime stats may be down in some places of the world, but within our teaching sanctuaries, crime is most certainly up.

As a victim, I have been pulled toward both sides on the issue of guns. Shortly after the shooting of my father, then-Wisconsin Governor Tommy Thompson signed into law a bill that banned guns in schools and promoted tougher consequences.

"The senseless murder of Wauwatosa West Associate Principal Dale Breitlow made it only too clear that we must do more to make our schools safe. That's why I am proposing a tough new mandatory minimum prison sentence for anyone who commits a crime with a gun in or around a school. No excuses, no exceptions. And if you even bring a gun to school, you will lose your driver's license, too."

At the time, this was serious change. That these consequences now look like a slap on the wrist speaks to how much change has occurred in less than a generation. Nowadays, most schools, including elementary schools, require students and visitors to pass through metal detectors. People are required to wear ID badges and schools regularly practice lockdown drills. In public school settings, there are new dress codes. Instead of teachers gaining instruction on new teaching styles, they are now taught techniques on how to better confront students.[2]

Current school security measures would have been beyond foreign to me in the 1990s, yet are common today. I know these changes are not across the board in every school across the country, but they are clearly becoming more common.

The suggestions on the National Safety School Center website include lockdowns, dress codes, ID badges and metal detectors – which sounds more like a prison to me than a place to grow and mold the future of the world.

Ronald Stephens, executive director of the National School Safety Center, has what seems to be a very dark outlook of the school system, as listed on the organization's website (http://www.schoolsafety.us). He is quoted on the website and in a paper he wrote: "There are two types of school administrators: those who have faced a crisis and those who are about to."

What? If that is true, then we are in for an even darker future than any "Terminator" movie has portrayed. I know the man is paid to look for and prevent worst-case scenarios, but if crisis is inevitable in schools, perhaps we shouldn't even have schools. I refuse to accept this as a fact, instead choosing to believe that positive change is coming. I choose to believe our children have a safer and brighter future.

Indeed, the part most jolting aspect to me when I first read about these changes is how they ultimately take time away from teachers interacting with students. It's taking time away from educational preparations, continuing education, and how about just the process of spending limited time and energy – now replaced with teaching them how to confront students.

But what is to be done?

Associated Press education writer Kimberly Hefling is quoted in a PBS article stating: "Finding factors to blame, rightfully or not, is almost the easy part: bad parenting, easy access to guns, less value for the sanctity of life, violent video games, a broken mental health system. Stopping the violence isn't."

U.S. Education Secretary Arne Duncan was quoted that he believes schools are the safest place in a community and that the root cause of school-related violence is the easy access to guns. "This is a societal problem, it's not a school problem," said Duncan.

I used to agree with Mr. Duncan, that guns are the root cause of the problem. However, now I tend to agree more with Miss Helfing – up to a point.

That sentence in the PBS article, "Stopping the violence isn't," is where I disagree. This is where our conversation, and this book, ultimately will end. So let's explore why so many people, including the Education Secretary, believe the root of the problem simply begins and ends with guns.

The conversation with guns is not as much about the gun itself or even the type of gun, but more about gun access. Thus the conversation, "What to do about guns?" essentially can be broken down into two oversimplified statements: Allow for a gun in everyone's hand. That way, anybody who thinks about committing murder will think twice or be shot on site. Conversely, there's the argument to take away all guns. That way, there is no way anybody ever gets shot.

Logically, both of these statements make sense and can be answers, especially since the United States currently lives somewhere in between.

Yet both statements are fundamentally flawed. To elaborate for a moment, imagine we live in a perfect political world where Republicans and Democrats get along and hold hands on their way to Chipotle at lunchtime to cordially talk about compromise and respect for their opposing viewpoints.

After a round of organic vegetarian burritos, say these enlightened leaders magically agree and put a law into effect, in all states, at all levels of government. Instantly, we have legislation agreed upon by both sides of the conversation. Yay for utopian democratic government!

As an eternal optimist, I would like to think that something like this could happen. However, government leaders have demonstrated otherwise, as one disaster after another, followed by a terrorist attack then another school shooting after another natural disaster, on and on, lends itself to more rhetoric. More large-scale tragedy seemingly lends itself to more division, and in events that could be uniting us as humans instead create even more polarization.

Across the world and in the many variations of government that exist, I like to think that this country still has the most freedom and the greatest number of platforms for implementing change. I know it often doesn't seem that way, but the mere fact I wrote this book and you are reading it is partly testimony to that idea and cause for celebration. There is hope, so let's return to the issue at hand and the idea that we could have perfect-world democratic government finding common ground and a solution to gun legislation.

Scenario One: The case for more gun control – i.e. "Let's get rid of guns! Guns are bad!"

Imagine that today a law was passed that made all guns in the U.S. illegal. Not just the semi-automatic AK-47 type guns, but also handguns, rifles and shotguns. There is a conversation that can be had, which we are not going to get into, around banning specific gun types: meaning some guns are allowed while others are not based on fire rate, range and use . Instead we are just going to talk about guns as a whole and the law that magically went into effect making every type of gun illegal in this country.

To make this happen, a variety of things would have to shift in our collective consciousness. First of all, everybody would have to be cool letting the Second Amendment to the Constitution go by the wayside. If you aren't familiar with this amendment or the U.S. Constitution, it goes something like this: You have the right, as an American citizen, to keep and bear arms regardless of service in a militia.

The Second Amendment means that as of December 15, 1791, given a few basic criteria have been met, you as a law abiding citizen can own a piece of machinery that essentially was designed to inflict damage on another living sentient being—often with the intent to or resulting in killing it.

Second, people whose livelihoods revolve around gun usage would have their careers altered. These are people who make a living from or utilize the gun trade. Whether owning and operating a shooting range or living in the mountains hunting for dinner, you found a way to live your life in a reasonably similar and happy manner without a gun.

Guns even have a place on Wall Street, and a big one at that. If you are a stockbroker, you have the ability to trade companies that make guns. The likes of Sturm, Ruger & Co. (listed on the New York Stock Exchange as RGR) and Smith & Wesson (listed on the NASDAQ as SWHC) are traded millions of times each business day. Together, these two publicly traded companies have around a $2 billion market cap, meaning that they are worth about $2 billion bucks combined. Big business.

Personally, what this means for me is many of my extended family members who love to harvest deer in the Wisconsin winters for food and enjoy the camaraderie of the hunting experience would have to put down arms. I have known deer hunting as a family tradition as long as I have been alive.

Even though I don't dress up in blaze orange and sit in the forest for hours at a time waiting for a deer to come along while freezing off body parts (I really still don't see how is this fun, but my family and millions of others do), I do enjoy the rewards. There is nothing better to me than the taste and nourishment of an organically harvested deer. A friend of mine often described hunting as being at one with God walking amongst his creation – sort of like a scene from "Avatar." I see it as freezing my nuts off for God-knows-how-long, but I digress.

There are many other changes millions of people would have to make in their lives, such as sports (shooting is a part of both the Summer and

Winter Olympics), recreation (shooting ranges), and collections (ever been in a museum?). Not to mention alterations in how our law enforcement agencies operate.

The picture I am painting is one that is extreme. I get that. However, a move to either side is still a move. These moves often affect more people than we realize, for better or worse. When we have a conversation about changing how our government operates and how it changes policies, I believe it's important that we talk about all aspects and parties effected, whether it's in our own self-interest or not. It is just a conversation, so for the sake of the conversation, continue with me down the rabbit hole as we explore another world where everyone has a gun.

Scenario Two: The case for less gun control – i.e. "Let's make handguns accessible to everyone! Guns are good!"

Now imagine that today, a law magically passed that made all guns in the U.S. legal for everybody to own. This means semi-automatic weapons, rifles, handguns, and all the ones in between are available to anyone for their own preservation of life, freedom and property.

In the United States, it is already very easy to obtain a handgun compared to other nations. This is partly due to the centuries we have been accustomed to the aforementioned Second Amendment. In our example, though, we moved all the way to the other side of the spectrum. Now all the rules for carrying a handgun in public, which vary by local jurisdiction and state, are waved. Any restrictions on who may purchase handguns and how long they have to wait are now gone.

As of 2007, the U.S. was the most heavily armed country in the world, with what I thought was a staggering ninety guns for every one hundred citizens. That number now edges close to 100 percent with this new law in effect. If you think about it, it's likely there would be more guns in circulation than human beings in the United States with this policy change.[3]

This side of the conversation also means moving things in a direction where grandmas, pilots and elementary school teachers routinely have access to side arms. It means that fundamentally, many people are again having changes in how they look at guns in and around their life. People who previously had no training with guns are seeking out safety lessons and becoming comfortable holding a machine that is designed to take life, with the goal to preserve the life of the person standing behind it.

This side of the conversation means that everyone in the country embraces the Second Amendment and likes the idea of their neighbor having a gun. Or perhaps doesn't like their neighbor, and carries a gun for that reason.

There are places in this country already that are moving in this direction. As of this writing, the cities of Virgin, Utah, and Spring City, Utah, either have laws or strong city suggestions to put a gun in everyone's hands. Both of these cities are small, populations of around 1,000, and both are attempting to stamp out crime with guns.

Spring City and Virgin implemented gun safety programs as part of this shift. The mayor of Spring City defended his town's laws (legislative suggestions) in an interview on Fox News. In the interview, he talked about how he didn't think a Sandy Hook would happen in his town because everyone would be ready. Basically, he was saying, school shootings won't happen here, not on my dime.

The truth is there are no huge changes that need to be made to U.S. law with this side of the conversation. Yes, the U.S. lives somewhere in between the two extremes. But as you make guns accessible to more people, this means you are generally relaxing the research that goes into how people get guns. Simply put, more guns in circulation means more people have access to guns.

Personally, I have often thought about, but never been able to take, a gun safety class. I even enrolled and paid a deposit on a class once only to chicken out at the last moment. The idea of holding an implement that was so similar to the one that took my dad's life is something I just can't push past. If this were to become a reality, most people would be taking a gun into the workplace. Would I ultimately be comfortable as a gun-toting chiropractor? It's hard to fathom.

Compromise

The picture I hope I have painted is that moving in either direction in large increments isn't a great option for a variety of reasons. But my family has a saying, and let's at least be realistic, that if change were to happen around gun control, it's going to happen via incremental changes in incremental places.

That means states like Colorado, which happens to be a hotbed for this conversation due to multiple shootings in multiple locations, are likely to be the first to change in one direction or another. With so much pressure on politicians in both parties, something legislative is liable to happen eventually.

So how does incremental progress with all factions in agreement change the overall violence quotient? Likely the answer is minimally.

Turning the dial one way or another might make one side of the conversation happy. But if history is worth noting, implementing more rules, regulations and changes likely isn't going to make a difference.

Even if I am wrong, and I would be thrilled to be wrong, the bottom line is we are still not at this statistic: zero shooting-related deaths.

Let's say that gun legislation changes and the violence stat now reads for the better, i.e. murders decrease the few years post-gun legislation change. The number still not seen is zero. This is the number I wish to see posted in Colorado, Washington, D.C., Chicago, or well, anywhere.

If we are not having a conversation with guns and there is no new crazy Jetson-esque future out there for the world where guns can magically be detected across all spectrums, what are we talking about?

I recently spoke with my aunt about this book, and as she works for the prison system, she is an excellent source for me. I asked her what she recalled about Leonard and him having a gun, and she stated simply: "Jay, there was no reason for Leonard to *not* have a gun."

This means that despite being expelled from high school and law enforcement officials responding with force, he had every right to a gun.

Would my father being armed have saved his life? Perhaps. Would you want your children's principal carrying a gun at all times? Doubtful, but some people do. Had metal detectors and badges been in place, would a school-related shooting have been prevented? Perhaps. Would Leonard have found another way to take my father's life, like in the parking lot, or worse, at home with his family present, as he originally planned? Likely.

There is no answer to the gun debate that will make everyone happy, and likely there is no law written at any moment in time past or future that even satisfies 51 percent of Americans. Instead, I believe that in order to be a country with zero gun-related deaths, there needs to be a series of changes across everyone's consciousness that can and ultimately will lead us to live a life where we can walk down any alley and be comfortable.

There is no one solution out there, and the problem is by talking about guns at all, we are having the wrong conversation. We are asking the wrong questions.

<u>Sources</u>

1. Marquette University Libraries; Tommy G. Thompson Collection: Gubernatorial Speeches.
2. *Salt Lake Tribune*, "Despite increased security, school shootings continue," Associated Press, February 2, 2014.
3. "U.S. most armed country with 90 guns per 100 people," by Laura MacInnis, Aug. 28, 2007, Reuters.com

Statistics:

"Gun Control Facts," by James D. Agresti and Reid K. Smith. Just Facts, September 13, 2010. Revised 2/11/2013.

Chapter 5

Creating a Violent Mind

"Finding factors to blame, rightfully or not, is almost the easy part: bad parenting, easy access to guns, less value for the sanctity of life, violent video games, a broken mental health system."
Fed 2014, AP News

Finding problems is never the hard part of reporting or writing. Many people can find problems with the world just having a dinner conversation. Have you ever spoken with someone and all they did was tell you what was wrong with someone or something? Ask them how they suggest to fix it and they shrug their shoulders.

I'm interested in solutions. But before we can present solutions, I believe it's better to have a firm grasp of a problem's fundamentals.

For instance, anybody working an algebra equation has to have a basic understanding of the concepts of moving around variables, adding, subtracting and dividing. Anybody can look at an equation, move around some numbers or letters and say, "Here's a solution," while ignoring the fundamentals. That doesn't mean it's right.

A proper solution approach requires understanding the fundamentals of the problem in addition to considering what solutions may look like. When you look at the fundamentals of any problem, be it algebra, a noisy neighbor or violent behavior, solutions, and therefore goals, become easier to grasp when you recognize the core problem.

Let's start with mental health. Part of the reason this is relevant to the conversation is because Leonard was diagnosed as a schizophrenic. Whether intentional or not, a large number of surviving perpetuators of violence either plead to insanity or attempt to play an insanity-defense card.

Many perpetrators of significant violence simply kill themselves, leaving little to learn about who they were and why they did what they did. However, I think it would be safe to say that when a shooter takes their life, there is some mental instability involved. Often in a case of mental stability, the individual likely would have written out a plan and verbalized a reason why they did what they did and who it was aimed at. Yet overwhelmingly, this is not the case.

CBS's *60 Minutes* addressed this exact topic on January 26, 2014, in a segment entitled "Nowhere to Go: Mentally Ill Youth in Crisis." Scott Pelley reported on the current shortcomings of mental health care for young people in the U.S.

Virginia State Senator Creigh Deeds and his late 24-year-old son, Gus Deeds, were the focus of the story. The story begins with archived footage of college-aged Gus being active with his father's election campaign. It portrays him as a good student at the well-respected College of William & Mary, where he played music – loved music, in fact – had many friends and was socially accepted.

Then, almost out of the blue, after his father's campaign was over, Gus became a shell of his former self. He grew anti-social, stopped taking care of himself, dropped out of school and chose to not keep a job. Eventually he was diagnosed with bipolar disorder.

His father told *60 Minutes* he was so worried Gus would kill himself that he got rid of all the guns in their rural Virginia farmhouse, except one hunting rifle that had no ammunition. With the bipolar disorder confirmed and medication starting, Gus eventually returned to William and Mary – at least for a short while.

When Gus became unstable again, the Deeds family discovered merely "talking to somebody" and getting treatment is harder in mental health than any other type of medicine. Part of the reason? Well, sometime around 1960, many of the large mental institutions began closing, which ultimately left people with acute mental health issues nowhere to go. *60 Minutes* stated the number of beds available for the mentally ill dropped from 500,000 to less than 100,000 over a period of roughly fifty years.

That left the Deeds family, along with many families, with only one option: the emergency room. Here was a father with a great love for his child, who had spent many loving hours with him, supporting his future and his goals, knowing something wasn't right. Gus was on prescription medication, sometimes taking it and sometimes not. When things continued to get worse, the Deeds family went to the local hospital. It was their only option, and if nothing else, at least it was a safe option.

That is when things got frightening for the family. A representative of the county agency that manages mental health care told Sen. Deeds that he couldn't find a hospital with a psychiatric bed appropriate for Gus' case.

Here is a conversation between *60 Minutes* reporter Scott Pelley and Sen. Deeds:

Scott Pelley: You're concerned that your son is suicidal. The clock has run out on the emergency room and he comes in and says, "Sorry, you've got to leave?"

Creigh Deeds: Well, he said that Gus wasn't suicidal. I guess he'd made …

Pelley: Based on his evaluation.

Deeds: His evaluation that Gus wasn't suicidal.

Pelley: What did you say to him, in leaving the emergency room?

Deeds: I said, "The system failed my son tonight."

For the Deeds family, with no resources and no idea how to treat mental illness, there was no place to go but home. The very next day, a clearly unstable Gus Deeds attacked his father with a knife, permanently scarring his face, and then shot himself with the only gun left on the family farm. Young Gus had thought about the event beforehand and planned the details. Gus was able to purchase ammunition secretly for the one gun left in the house – the one without ammunition his father had deemed safe.

The story left me moved for a variety of reasons. First, this young man reminded me so much of a young Leonard McDowell. They were both, at least at one point in their lives, stable enough to be enrolled in school and active in social scenes. Account after account from Leonard's former classmates indicates he was "strange," if nothing else. I will concede that perhaps he wasn't as social as Gus Deeds.

It is conceivable that Gus Deeds could have been guided by voices in his head, much like Leonard stated he had been. Leonard felt he had to get even, and perhaps Gus felt the same. Had Gus followed a different, more violent, train of thought the day he decided to attack his father, the outcome could have been much worse, including endangering the general public. Perhaps part of the reason this case wasn't ultra-high profile and I had never heard of it prior to *60 Minutes*, is in the end, it was labeled only as a suicide.

The National Institute of Mental Health states that over the last ten years, between 40 percent and 50 percent of people with serious mental disorders are left untreated in the U.S. That means on any given day, there are up to 3.5 million adults with schizophrenia or bipolar disorder not being treated. I don't want to throw too much sand at this stat, as oftentimes treatment is just drug therapy. I'll have more on drug therapy later and why I believe it's only a stopgap solution.

The second reason I was moved by the Deeds family's situation was the fact they pursued every option they knew about. The avenues to get help were followed and at least some help was given – albeit very little and clearly not enough to save a life.

This is the difference between Leonard and Gus. Leonard, to my knowledge, wasn't monitored or helped to nearly the same extent. Gus was. Yet the objective was similar, to hurt another person.

I am quite certain no parent ever sets out to be a bad. Yes, there are the stories of some overwhelmed parents who dispose of their babies in Dumpsters and do other terrible things. However, let's look at those cases at outliers and focus on the majority for this topic. The article written by the Associated Press' Helfing in Chapter 4 states "bad parenting" is an obvious problem. I would choose to use a different phrase: "Challenging family dynamics are an obvious problem."

This sentence covers parents who, yes, are "bad at parenting." It also covers children who, for whatever reason, live in a situation where dynamics strain the ability to benefit from appropriate mentorship. Be it financial, societal, health concerns, divorce, fighting or just plain ambivalence, even the best-intentioned parents can be labeled as bad – which is again why I prefer the phrase "challenging family dynamics."

As far as I can tell, Gus Deeds was the recipient of love from his family and his father, "but sometime after his father's loss in that governor race and his parents' subsequent divorce in 2010, the younger Deeds fell into a downward spiral of mental illness." [1]

Studies have begun to surface that show links between a child's mental stability and divorced parents. The studies categorize these children as being generally more mentally unstable then their age-related peers. The studies suggest it is inevitable that with divorce comes dispute, and with that, children are frequently forced into the position of playing an adult role years before they are ready. We have all seen a movie where a child is asked, forced or tricked into playing the role of messenger, judge, jury, spy, patient or even witness.

First documented in a 2005 study:

Children whose parents... divorce, exhibit higher levels of anxiety/depression and antisocial behavior than children whose parents remain married. There is a further increase in child anxiety/depression but not antisocial behavior associated with the event of parental divorce itself. [2]

Additional research echoes these findings: "Children of divorced parents often fall behind their classmates in math and social skills and are more likely to suffer anxiety, stress and low self-esteem." Researcher Hyun Sik Kim, of the University of Wisconsin, said the study showed the detrimental effects on the children do not start until after the parents begin divorce proceedings.

He attributed developmental setbacks of the children to several factors, including the stress of living with bickering and potentially depressed parents, unstable living arrangements, dividing time between parents in separate homes, and economic hardship from a drop in family income.

I contend these developmental setbacks of bickering parents, depressed parents, economic hardship and unstable living environments can just as easily be present within a marriage as well. The stress of splitting time between parents could be akin to the stress of a married parent that travels frequently for work.

Witnessing the loss of love between parents, having parents break their marriage commitment, adjusting to going back and forth between two different households, and the daily absence of one parent while living with the other are all potentially challenging circumstances. In the personal history of the child, parental divorce is a watershed event. Life that follows is significantly changed from how life was before.[3]

This is true for most divorces, as there are no doubt massive changes brought into the child's life no matter what their age. But the change doesn't have to be bad, per se. Watershed, perhaps, but I wouldn't necessarily label it instantly as "bad."

Simply stating "divorce" as a cause for challenging family dynamics isn't telling the whole story. All of the above research and quotes are valid – to an extent. As an outsider to divorce looking in, I'm saying, "Hey, I have gone through all those things," yet my parents were never divorced. Divorce in itself doesn't have to be the negative event the statisticians make it seem; nor is staying married through what can be gigantic emotional storms always a positive event. Is it potentially traumatic for everyone involved? Clearly. Does it require making family dynamics more challenging? Absolutely not.

I never really understood what to say to some of my friends in high school, or at any other time for that matter, when they told me their parents were getting a divorce. "I'm sorry," "Oh, that's unexpected," "Want to play video games?" "Should we get a drink?" are just a few of the awkward pre- and post-pubescent reactions that spewed from my mouth. Likely the better response would have been, "Is there anything I can do to help?"

Divorce can be a good thing for the family's dynamic. It can create an environment that is more stable for children. It may liberate young minds from a house that is otherwise filled with bickering, fighting and yelling. It's more likely that remaining in an environment filled with daily unhappiness is far more damaging to children that the divorce itself.

Life changes and life evolves. This is true for all people. In the context of marriage, what is more important is not whether parents divorce or not, but the environment your children are placed into on a regular basis. If divorce is best for a couple, so be it. What matters going forward is how you speak and act as a former couple. You may no longer love your ex, but your children do.

Any parent speaking negatively about another parent around a child, whether married or not, will create a huge amount of anxiety and confusion. It was love that brought your children into the world, and it is love, kindness and patience that will nurture them. It is not a question of whether or not children experience storms in life. The question is how they weather the inevitable storms of life.

Love will lend itself to stability across all arenas. This includes, but is certainly not limited to, mental stability, physical fitness, personal growth and acceleration in the classroom. This, in turn, will have our children paying it forward to their classmates, friends and random people they meet on the street. Who knows, it could lend itself to inviting a stranger met at a fish fry in for dinner one night!

The studies on divorce may be true, but they are true in a narrow context. The studies, in my estimation, are better suited to looking at a broader context: How much love does a child get on a daily basis? Looking at the above studies, almost every single citation associated with divorce could be framed another way. The "divorce studies" could just as easily focus on married parents who are constantly fighting or yelling at their children. I doubt a study of this magnitude and scope is out there, but anecdotally, I do believe this to be true: A loving home of any kind is what matters most.

"A person who has a secure relationship with a parent is more likely than someone who is insecure to feel that they can trust the parent," said R. Chris Fraley, associate professor at the University of Illinois at Urbana-Champaign and co-author of the study on parent psychology.[4] "Such a person is more comfortable depending on the parent and is confident that the parent will be psychologically available when needed."

This is an interesting study. What the author is saying is parents are mentors and developing minds need mentorship. I assert that yes, normally, a parent fills a role as confidant, but a parent doesn't need to be the exclusive provider of that role. My father was my role model and best friend, but his mentorship disappeared in the blink of an eye. This was devastating to our family and me, and the repercussions could have been much worse. Toss me into any divorce study because we had "challenging family dynamics" for certain.

Yes, *60 Minutes* got it right. There is a huge problem with respect to acute mental health cases. But one of the most frustrating things about watching *60 Minutes* is the show rarely – if ever – gives any solutions. I get it, their job is investigative reporting, but if you are like me, you watch shows like these and want to help. How about a link to a Facebook action group or a charity to support, at a minimum? Bringing a problem to the forefront solves one great problem of creating awareness, but 99 percent of something done is still 100 percent unfinished.

The *60 Minutes* episode finished with this from Senator Deeds: "I want people to remember the brilliant, friendly, loving kid that was Gus Deeds. We'll use Gus, I hope, to address mental health and to make sure that other people don't have to suffer through this."

Added Pelley, "The state of Virginia is investigating why there was no hospital bed for Gus Deeds that night. Nationwide, since 2008, states have cut $4.5 billion from mental health care funding."

And that's it. End of episode.

Wait a minute, that's it? I mean, you leave people thinking, "Oh well, I guess the state is on it." Or "$4.5 billion is a lot of coin; we aren't ever going to be able to get over that hump."

As an aside, the estimated cost of the wars in Iraq and Afghanistan was nearing $3 trillion by the end of 2013's fiscal year. Some estimates have the wars reaching $4 trillion. If we take the lower number, that means we are spending nearly 700 times more money shooting people in other countries than investing into one state's mental health program.

Let's play with that stat for a bit. Let's say the government is going to invest $4.5 billion for each state to work on mental health. That totals around $225 billion dollars. I understand mental health resources and finances will be different in North Dakota versus California, but let's just use these numbers for a minute. A $225 billion nationwide mental-health program is expensive, no doubt, and that money isn't just lying around in Washington. But let's just say that came out of the budget from current overseas wars. That still barely makes a dent in the $2 to $4 trillion dollars we have chosen to spend on our national security in Iraq and Afghanistan.

To further the financial conversation, in March of 2013, then-Mayor Michael Bloomberg and Mayors Against Illegal Guns, a political action group of 1,000-plus U.S. mayors, was beginning a $12 million television ad blitz. The commercials were set to run in key states to push for closing some of the loopholes that exist for purchasing guns. Yep, that's $12 million bucks on TV ads to further the gun debate; which will likely, if not inevitably, lead to more money spent by the National Rifle Association (NRA) to counter these commercials.

The NRA has, at least in its estimation, won every gun battle it has ever faced. Just in time for the 2014 political season, Mr. Bloomberg doubled down and joined forces with Moms Demand Action for Gun Sense in America. The Moms group was founded shortly after the school shootings in Newtown, Connecticut, in 2012. These two groups merged into the Everytown for Gun Safety coalition.

In fact, these concerned parents and mayors are quadrupling down and spending a reported $50 million in ads to force the gun debate to the front of the political scene ... again. The group's cause is noble; I have been there. I supported this debate once myself. The problem is they are using fear as their ally, just as the NRA is.

Mr. Bloomberg uses phrases like, "This new organization will bring more people into the fight against gun violence, which affects every town in America." If that isn't fighting fire with fire – or in this case, guns with guns, I don't know what is. Speaking almost like a prizefighter egging on his opponent, Bloomberg says, "We've got to make them [the NRA] afraid of us." This is not love speaking. This is not how compromise is made or how the sanctity of life is honored.

Nobody wants another Newtown. Not the NRA nor the anti-gun groups. Let's start by asking different questions, beginning on the same page. I bet a billion bucks that if you poll everyone in the NRA and the Everytown for Gun Safety group, the results to the question: Would you like to see another school shooting, ever? The results would be unanimously no.

In my opinion, criminals will always be able to get their hands on guns. Overwhelmingly, people who have been characterized as "criminals," in fact, do not carry out gun violence in school settings. Period. Instead, nearly every person to carry out school violence, or even a mass shooting like the movie theatre in suburban Denver in 2012, was or can be classified as mentally ill.[5]

The Mayors against Illegal Guns and the Moms Against Guns groups may have been focused initially on safety, but that call to action has been clouded. If, indeed, the goal is different, it seems the phrase, "I can't hear what you are saying because your actions are speaking so loud," rings true.

Imagine if the $62 million in ad campaigns had been spent on the mental and social health of our children rather than anti-gun messages. Money spent talking about guns furthers the debate, and if nothing else, can make guns seem sexier for the people who aren't supposed to have them. Have you ever seen a sign that says "Please don't touch?" What's the first thing you want to do? Touch whatever it is!

There is a gun for nine out of ten people in this country. Realistically, if somebody wants a gun badly enough, it doesn't matter the age or mental ability, they will be able to get a gun. Putting together an anti-gun campaign is like putting a big "Do not touch" sign on guns. The movie and book The Secret by Rhonda Byrne does a magnificent job talking about using the affirmative of a phrase.

For example, she cites anti-war protestors and pro-peace demonstrators generally want the exact same thing. But guess what, the anti-war protests often turn violent and the scene appears like a war. Instead the pro-peace rally generally has colors, lively music and sometimes mind-altering drugs. Just saying … I know what party I want to be at. So with that in mind, how can we create minds that are less violent and more loved?

Sources

1. "Friends Saw Creigh Deeds' Son Struggle With Bipolar Disorder Before Killing," ABC News Nov. 21, 2013, by Abby D. Phillip, Serena Marshall and Jim Avila.

2. Parental Divorce and Child Mental Health Trajectories Lisa Strohschein[*]. Article first published online: 21 NOV 2005 DOI: 10.1111/j.1741-3737.2005.00217.x; *Journal of Marriage and Family*, Volume 67, Issue 5, pages 1286–1300, December 2005.

3. "The Impact of Divorce on Young Children and Adolescents - Young children and adolescents can respond differently to divorce," published December 19, 2011, by Carl E. Pickhardt, Ph.D in Surviving (Your Child's) Adolescence in *Psychology Today*. http://www.psychologytoday.com

4. "Children Of Divorce: Study Finds Younger Children Feel Lasting Effects Of Divorce," *Huffington Post*, posted: 07/01/2013, Associated Press.

5. "Mayors Against Illegal Guns To Launch Gun-Control Ad Blitz," *Huffington Post*. Michael Bloomberg, posted: 03/23/2013. Associated Press.

Chapter 6

Entertaining and Loving Your Brain

The night before Leonard McDowell allegedly took my father's life, he was watching an ultra-violent movie on television. Coincidentally, my parents were flipping through the tube that same night of November 30, 1993, and came across the same show. They paused for a moment on the channel, remarking to each other about why shows like this are on television at all. Then they moved on.

I recall my mother talking with her family about that movie several weeks later. She wondered out loud if that movie hadn't been on that night, if things would have been different. The movie may have given Leonard some violent courage, sure, but the likely answer is "no." However, it begs a question: How is entertainment shaping our future minds?

There is little doubt the video game and movie industry has moved significantly in the direction of greater detail and higher resolutions. TVs at home are larger and reveal more details than ever before. Blu-ray discs create a stunning clarity and show the viewer even more details. The technology is also becoming cheaper and widely available to everyone. Think about this:

For $200, you can get a Blu-ray player and 24-inch TV delivered to your home in two days with free shipping.

I know, 24 inches for a TV is small by today's standards, yet this example stands as one that demonstrates just how easy it is for most everybody to have access to a very detailed viewing experience.

Case in point, my wife and I were watching *Hotel Rwanda* the other night, which incidentally is an incredibly moving film based on a true story of the Rwandan genocide.

Hotel Rwanda came out in 2004, a short ten years ago from this writing. At one point near the start of the movie, there is a car scene where you can tell the background is not real. It isn't bad cinematography by any means. At the same time, you don't have to stretch your imagination to see it is a superimposed background. Christina looked at me and said, "It looks so fake." To which I responded, "It just goes to show you how far entertainment has come in a short time."

We expect all our movies nowadays to look real, and anything that is not likely will be seen right away on the high-definition screen. Incredible graphics, expensive scenery and new technology have changed everything. Yet for all the wonderful sensory experiences Hollywood and technology engineers across the world have created, there is a consequence. The consequence is gore and violence are more real and detailed than ever.

Take the 2013 movie *Django Unchained.* My wife and I went to see the movie after having heard about the incredible writing and that it had been nominated for several Academy Awards, including Best Picture. What we didn't know was just how violent, bloody and graphic it was. Now don't get me wrong, it was a well-written movie and did have an excellent story. Yet if you have seen the movie, you know there is blood, guts and shooting in one scene after another after another.

For some people, I imagine this doesn't matter to them and it is part of the cinematic experience – and I agree to an extent. I admit when I was watching *Hotel Rwanda*, I felt for a moment like I was watching an old black-and-white Western. That is how much things have changed.

Going back about two decades and contrasting *Django* with the 1993 Academy Awards makes it even clearer. The 1993 Best Picture nominees included *The Pianist, Schindler's List, In the Name of the Father, The Remains of the Day* and lastly and most violently *The Fugitive*.

The Fugitive perfectly illustrates my point. The plot depends on Harrison's Ford's character, Richard Kimble, being wrongly imprisoned as a murderer. In this movie, the entire plot is centered on the murder of Richard's wife. The movie shows the murder scene more than once, but by today's standards it is extraordinarily PG-rated. Does it change the movie experience for anybody involved? Do we lose any sense of how important that scene is to the outcome of the movie by not actually seeing the gruesome details? I vote no.

The contrast again is *Django*. In this movie, death is part of the plot and vital to the storyline. The main character, Django, is attempting to save his wife from a brutal slave owner. The difference is when death is relative to the story, instead of just a small clip, there is blood everywhere with each killing. And I do mean everywhere! Even look at the DVD cover or the IMDb.com promo photos. Jamie Foxx, who plays the hero, Django, has blood splattered on his back. You needn't even watch the movie to see your first blood bath.

I hear the counterargument: "What about the other 2013 Best Picture nominees?" There are some nonviolent films such as *Amour* and *Silver Linings Playbook,* which were also nominated for Best Picture, and perhaps *Django* is an outlier. Perhaps not, as one of the other nominees, *Zero Dark Thirty,* includes torture scenes, violent bombing, as well as kill scenes. Just one snapshot of how far we can drift in twenty short years is that we have come to accept and perhaps even expect blood to be in our films. In fact, the movie rating service IMDb.com now includes a parents' resource section giving films a score of how violent they are on a 1 to 10 scale.

The same can be said for video games. Coincidentally, in 1993 there was a shift beginning to occur in the content of material we put in front of our children for entertainment. I'm talking about the advent of the gore in video games, and I was front and center for the unveiling. My two favorite games at the time, *Street Fighter II* and *Mortal Combat*, had just been released. Their popularity and style changed everything. I would sit for hours on end – literally hours after school – playing one if not both of these games. If you are unfamiliar with this type of game platform, it's essentially a two-person fight scene, you versus another human or computer, depending if you have a friend with you.

Instead of honing my algebra skills or reading about Booker T. Washington, I was obsessed with learning how to better destroy my opponent and move on to the next level. There is a still famous line in *Mortal Combat* when you are done defeating your opponent that sums it all up: "Finish him."

What happens next when you're about to beat the other guy? He just sits there, essentially lifeless, waiting for you to come along and deliver the final blow. The game is already over, but for effect, your character walks up and gets extra points by ripping out the other dude's spine, punching his head off or pulling his heart out.

Our goal with the entire game was to get to the point where we were rewarded extra points, not for style, but for killing the person. Yep. You heard that right. As a 15-year-old, hormone-filled, high-school kid, I thought nothing of it. My goal was to survive school, come home, flip on the Super NES (our slang for the Super Nintendo Entertainment System) and rip dudes' spines out. Thinking about that wasted time in my youth to this day fills me with a deep sadness.

The contrast is that five years earlier, one of the first video games with violence was "Mike Tyson's Punch-Out!!" The style is similar in that it's a "you versus another guy" fight platform. The difference is at the end of the game, if you beat Mike Tyson, there is no message to kill the guy. In fact, at the end of the match, the message from Tyson is, "Great fighting. You were tough, Mac." A nice, positive comment reminding the player that it's a sport. Then, "I've never seen such finger speed" to remind the gamer it's a video game. There was no actual physical fight.

Of course, after Dad passed away and my entire world had changed, "finishing anybody" lost its appeal. Personally, I began to think about things differently, in a more human way so to speak. I began to think about how ludicrous these games are. Slowly, my consciousness started to change. Video games became less and less a part of my life.

Do we really know how many 15-year-old kids are being shaped by these video games and movies that are standing on the other side of the gun? How much of our collective consciousness has come to accept violence and death as commonplace? Perhaps we can't tangibly answer that question – at least not yet – but we can start asking questions and raising our consciousness.

What is known without doubt is video games now are significantly more advanced, detailed and graphic. I remember when I was in sixth grade, around 1990, and the Super NES first came out, it was all the rage. I remember my teacher, Mr. Benson, saying to us, "That's great, you guys, but I hear someday you will be able to see fingers move and I tell you what, I am waiting for that day."

I thought to myself, "That is absurd! Fingers moving? I mean, I can almost make out a pixel for an eye, and '3' for a hand. But a finger? He's crazy." But here we are.

Today's video game market has become even larger and bigger than anybody could have imagined. Game manufactures are traded on the stock markets, as are retailers and distributors. One of the largest computer makers in the world, Microsoft, is part of the prestigious thirty companies in the Dow Jones Industrial Average. Yet oftentimes when analysts talk about the growth of Microsoft, the growth is in respect to its video game division currently known as Xbox. Without Xbox, Microsoft would be considered "old tech."

We have even moved past the point where you need to go to the store to pick up a game to put in your console. Everything is downloadable, and you can play much more advanced games than *Street Fighter II* with somebody anywhere in the world. It's a world into which I have not stepped foot for some time, but knowing what gaming was like, I can only imagine how this is changing the youth of America, if not the world.

Video game releases have advanced to the point where they are advertised with the biggest sporting events in our culture. In fact, recently while watching a pro football playoff game, a commercial came on with a

Norse Viking singing a love song. The tune is in the nature where a guy is singing with a buddy, "It's such a perfect day; it's such a perfect day to spend with you." However, as the guy is singing, he is morphing from a Norse cutting off one guy's head to smashing his car in a high-speed chase to being at war, trying to shoot another dude. I mean, that is insane, right? Love music set to the tone of World War V?

With respect to the Gus Deeds story from Chapter 5, local Virginia news affiliate WTVR mentioned – almost in passing – that Gus liked to play a fantasy game called *Morrowind* and a first-shooter (gun-fighting style) game called *Tribes Ascend*.[1]

As I was watching *60 Minutes*, I actually looked over at my wife and said, "I bet you there were video games in this young man's life." Without knowing the diagnosis and without having an idea of the medication he was on, I would be willing to bet the diagnoses included some form of Attention Deficit Disorder (ADD) and Attention Deficit Hyperactivity Disorder (ADHD) made worse by video games.

There is an effect to all this violence. The man who details it best is Daniel Amen, M.D., CEO of the Amen Clinics. In his brilliant book, *A Magnificent Mind at Any Age*, Dr. Amen talks about video-game culture and exactly what it is doing to the mind of youth. He details two studies from the University of Missouri that found real-life simulation video game play, like *Mortal Combat*, was positively related to aggressive behavior and delinquency.

Essentially, he found that the more time kids spent on video games, the more trouble they had in school. This means there is a direct correlation to lowered performance in school studies as the mind is on a screen. Another of the studies detailed how there is a direct correlation between time spent on video games and both long- and short-term aggressive behavior. Dr. Amen has reviewed dozen of studies, and the findings repeat again and again: exposure to violent video games is significantly linked to increases in aggressive behavior, aggressive thoughts, aggressive feelings and cardiovascular arousal.

To me, the most interesting finding is this exposure to video games also decreases helping (servant) behavior. When researchers identify a direct link from something that essentially moves humans to help other humans *less*, I believe this could – or perhaps should – be national news. Sadly, it is not … at least yet.

"It's generally accepted that the average American spends more time watching TV than the average person from any other country… and some Americans watch upward of five hours of TV a day."[2] Yet, I recently discovered that might be changing. An article on theatlantic.com details "screen time" across the world. The results were, to me, unexpected.

According to the article, the United Kingdom has now slipped into first place, with the average daily time the television is on besting the U.S. by one minute for a grand total of 148 daily minutes. Basically, two and a half hours a day spent staring at a screen. The article goes on to detail PC usage, led by China at 161 minutes a day, and smartphone and tablet use. The world leader in smartphone screen time? Nigeria. Yep, Nigeria leads the pack at 193 minutes per day. Over three hours per day spent hooked up to smartphones. The U.S. had a miniscule, but still proud, 151 minutes daily spent on iPhones and other such devices.

My point in bringing these stats up is the U.S. is not alone in hooking up to technology. We are hooked up as a world, now more than ever. When I asked my best friend from high school, Brian, when he thought we plugged in, he gave his sad reply. He thought we were hooked up until we left for college. This was also my recollection. Although we had shifted from death-style games, we were playing football games, *Metroid*, and what we called "Kartathons." The Kart marathons were the hours on end we spent playing *Mario Kart*.

I told Brian that as long as I can, as long as she will let me, I will guide my daughter, Selom, away from video games. He has a three–year-old son and agrees with me wholeheartedly. In fact, a text message early in the morning from him kind of sums the whole thing up: "I think the Kartathons stopped the end of our senior year of high school. It still upsets me thinking about what we could have put all of the time into. Being able to hit the shortcut on Rainbow Road every time probably equates to being a concert violinist."

Brian is right, the hours spent on video games may have equated into a lifelong talent or even a career. My goal here is not to demonize video game culture or television. Neither one of these is the direct cause of violence in America. I just hope to create an awareness that it is easier now, more than any time in the history of the world, to get online and watch or play nearly anything.

But how is this affecting our brains? How is this shaping our future? I believe screen time and the repercussions of it consuming our lives is one aspect contributing to overall youth violence. Dr. Amen has a long list of examples. In the list below, he reviews other issues with regard to brain function that further impacts how our youth processes information.

Dr. Amen's 14 Bad Brain Habits That May Affect All Age Groups:

- Lousy diet
- Little exercise
- Risking brain trauma
- Chronic stress
- Negative thinking, chronic worry or anger
- Poor sleep
- Cigarette smoke
- Excessive caffeine
- Aspartame and MSG
- Exposure to environmental toxins
- Excessive TV time
- Excessive time playing video games
- Excessive computer time (also to be included here would be smart phone or tablet usage)
- More than a little alcohol

Prior to writing this book, I hadn't seen *Bowling for Columbine* by Michael Moore, but it seemed a very appropriate research topic. If you haven't seen the movie, it's a very short and interesting watch, and I highly recommend it. There is a bit of a political bias in his documentaries, but just watch for the content with an open mind. It's worth it.

The plot of the movie centers on Michael Moore investigating why there is so much gun violence in America. Using the shooting at Columbine as his impetus for change, he confronts and interviews the likes of former NRA president Charlton Heston, corporate leaders of Kmart (where the ammunition for the Columbine attack was purchased), the writers for the show *South Park* and Gothic rock singer Marilyn Manson.

At the time of the shooting, the shooters were listening to lots of the dark music written by Marilyn Manson. Manson was labeled a villain as a catalyst for the violence. In fact, when Manson and his band came to Denver to play a concert a year later, it was a controversial news story.

The interesting thing about the list above, and everything I have read in studies, is music has been shown to have little or nothing to do with creating a violent mind. That's not to say it can't change a mood or give some courage to somebody who is about to create a violent event. Even Mr. Manson himself, when asked what he would say to the Columbine boys, had a very thoughtful and love-based response: "I wouldn't say a single word to them. I would just listen to what they have to say, and that's what no one did."

The research Dr. Amen has put together is staggering when you consider what this means for the future of our society as a whole. After reading his books and cruising around his website, it has vastly changed the way I eat, think, move and fill my brain.

Dr. Amen's work on the brain is principally focused on looking at the specifics of ADD and ADHD. He looks at the two as generally interchangeable and present in a lot more people than I had initially thought.

My wife, since I have known her, claimed she had ADD, and for years I blew her off. I said things such as, "Yeah, yeah. You are making this up and you know that is a garbage diagnosis anyways." Then one day, after going out on a long bike ride and listening to Dr. Amen's book, *Magnificent Mind at Any Age*, I realized I was terribly wrong.

The conversation went like this when I got home:

"Christina, I am so sorry, You were right."

"I know I'm right. I'm always right. What did you realize I'm right about?"

"Well, remember all these years you have told me you have ADD?"

"Mmmmmmhmmmmmm. I'm listening."

"Well, after listening to this book, it turns out you are right!"

"I told you I am right. I'm always right. Now can you take the trash out?"

Christina fit classically into one of Dr. Amen's six basic ADD subtypes. The best part was now that I was truly listening to her needs, we were able to start her on a couple of cheap supplements and augment her exercise routine to support the way her brain functions. The result was a more patient and understanding husband who comprehends his wife's thoughts, words and deeds better. In turn, I had a generally happier and more focused wife! Within a month of this discovery, we became pregnant and later gave birth to our first child.

ADD isn't a bad label; it's just a descriptor for how a person's brain functions. When you know how your brain functions and what keeps it focused, you can use it to its full potential. For most people, it's like the dogs in the Disney movie *Up*. If you haven't seen *Up* or have forgot about the dogs, there are some funny scenes where the dogs talk through the use of special collars. With the assistance of the collars, the dogs talk articulately with other dogs and people. Then, there's an instant where they catch sight of a squirrel. All of sudden, midsentence, they freeze, yell "Squirrel!" watch the squirrel run away, and then resume the sentence.

Ever been working diligently, have a quick thought off-topic and then pull up Google, email or make a phone call? This one fleeting "squirrel" thought totally changes what you were doing. That's one type of a very basic ADD. For the more violent mind, these "squirrel" distractors become a way of life and often become a self-perpetuating cycle. The first step toward fulfilling your mind's brilliant potential and achieving great things is to know if you have ADD or even a propensity for your attention to drift.

As a chiropractor, it is my belief that we are all designed by God to live our lives with a certain amount of potential. This potential differs from person to person based on their genetic structure, how and where they were raised, etc. Think about the nature versus nurture conversation. Irrespective of what you believe your potential and talents come from on the nurture versus nature spectrum, what is clear is we are all different.

For example, I am never going to run as fast a Usain Bolt. The guy is the world-record holder for the 100-meter dash at the highest of all competitive levels, the Olympics. Bolt was born with a genetic sequence that developed him tall and muscular, perfect for sprinting. Was he the most gifted sprinter ever born in the history of the world? Perhaps, but perhaps not. What Mr. Bolt has done in addition to his "God-given potential" is train, and he trains hard. Had he adopted a couch-potato lifestyle, he may still be an Olympic athlete, but certainly never an Olympic champion. It's fairly safe to say Usain Bolt, as an athlete, has fulfilled his potential.

We are all born with a potential inside us. As a chiropractor, my role is to facilitate the life experience and optimize people's potential life experiences. What Dr. Amen is doing is optimizing brain potential. He does a terrific job of dedicating his life to the human brain, and when you look at violent humans and the recurring patterns and characteristics of these people, there is an overwhelming presence of ADD/ADHD character traits.

The clinical side of what is going on with Dr. Amen and his clinics involves taking a person with basic ADD/ADHD traits and, after a thorough examination, performing a scan of the brain. Using a database of thousands of scans, he can identify which part of the brain is either under or over-firing. Along with the basic history (i.e. traumas and toxins) and the behavior pattern, a remedy can often be formed naturally.

Naturally means using a variety of amino acid supplements (which are generally very affordable and effective) and lifestyle alterations. There are also recommendations made for people who will respond better to pharmacologic interventions, such as people with bipolar or schizophrenia disorders. The list of brain diagnoses he has treated range from depression to PMS to obsessive-compulsive behavior. Many of his recommendations are cheap and natural.

Ultimately, where this work has the most applicability to the conversation about guns has to do with Dr. Amen's story about his nine-year-old nephew, Andrew. In an interview with *The Telegraph* he recounts the story:

"My nephew Andrew was nine when he attacked a girl for no reason. He would draw pictures where he was shooting other children. Now, if you don't look at his brain, you do what psychiatry has always done – blame the mother, or say that maybe someone's molesting him. But it's all just psychobabble. We looked at his brain and found a cyst the size of a golf ball in the left temporal lobe, which is often associated with violence." [4]

In *Magnificent Mind at Any Age*, Dr. Amen details how his sister-in-law, Sherrie, noticed how Andrew went from this sweet, loving child to somebody else. She knew her son so well that she recognized something was wrong! At this point in his still-young career, Dr. Amen's colleagues were extremely skeptical. Many were straight up hostile to him. But he pushed on for the love of his family and ultimately was able to diagnose the root cause of the problem.

I would have thought that once the problem was found, the Amen family would be able to simply have the cyst removed. However, the details of the story only further the challenges the family would have. In fact, this technology – and the idea of a cyst actually being operable and resolving mood issues – was something radical. Finally, with persistency, a good friend did the surgery. Once he removed the cyst, the behavior stopped, and Andrew and his family got their lives back. Modern psychiatry would have just thrown them on the trash.

I do think there is a real solution here in the future of brain analysis, and we will talk more about that in a minute. The captivating part of this story is how much one child's life changed because of who his uncle just happened to be. In my option, Dr. Amen is the world's leading expert on brain behavior and he *just happened* to be breaking in cutting-edge technology and linking them together. I mean, c'mon, how is that just coincidental? This was God's way of guiding the family. The love of Andrew's mother and uncle gave us the perfect example of how to live a life led by love and persistence.

When Dr. Amen needed to push the envelope and get out of the medical community's comfort zone, it was the association with family that provided the impetus. I don't have a personal association with the man, but I am convinced that had an unrelated nine-year-old boy showed up needing the same intervention, this boy's outcome would not have been the same.

Elaborating on his story about Andrew, Dr. Amen draws a comparison to this story and the need for "maverick thinking." Maverick thinking is essentially thinking out of the box to beat and deviate from the current standard. At the time, the standard with psychology was not to use technology; that the cyst was present but the surgery was considered just as harmful, if not more so due to its infancy as a treatment, as the cyst itself.

Yet in his gut, he knew he could help. The love for his nephew was the motivation that drove his maverick thinking and desire to create change. Without the meaningful connection to family, without the love for a nephew, it would have been easy for Dr. Amen to say, "Well, here is what we have done and had results with. Take these drugs/supplements and let's follow up in two months."

Then two months becomes six months. The drugs cover up some of the anger issues, and although the non-familiar version of Andrew is not nearly his old self, he is technically clinically improved. So the six months turn into an adolescence of anger and frustration, as mother and son fight about taking the drugs and going to school and slipping grades. When does it end? Or an even more chilling question, how does it end?

I maintain there are thousands of Andrew-type cases out there in the world. By this, I mean a very logical and simple fix to an otherwise unhealthy, underperforming brain just in need of guidance. Dr. Amen and his work remains cutting edge. It very well might be a long-term solution for ADD, ADHD, violence and anger. But until the technology to look at brain function is affordable for the entire country, we are left with only a small portion of the population who are able to undergo testing.

Perhaps an answer is to invest millions of dollars into a program where all children have access to a regional brain-scanning center. As radical as it sounds, perhaps it's not. There is currently a standard for screening women over 50 for breast cancer through the use of small, focused x-rays. Commonly, this technology is referred to as mammography. Back in the 1970s, this technology was new. Although not yet perfect, it has become widely used and accepted around the world. The screening test is inexpensive and requires little to no prep. Who's to say brain-scanning technology can't go through a similar evolution? It can.

I have spent a good amount of time wondering just what was going on in Leonard's brain that caused him to "lose it." As part of the trial, the defense attorney argued that part of Leonard's motivation for killing my father stemmed from the day he was expelled. Leonard didn't want to leave school, if you recall, and as part of his forceful evacuation, allegedly one of the police officers hit Leonard's head against the floor.

There were police and other teachers present. But my father, in his mind, was to blame because he called the police. Over and over, Leonard would talk and think about how this event embarrassed him and caused a "fissure" in his brain. What would a scan reveal about how well his brain was actually functioning? What would it tell us today?

It isn't fair for me to assume what the home life looked like for Leonard McDowell. His family may have loved him just as much as Andrew's. There is an ocean of change and evolution in twenty years' time, so let's just focus on the success of the Amen family.

The success of the Amen family is in one of the most basic and most powerful of human emotions: Love. Andrew's mother loved him so much that she couldn't stand to watch him become somebody he was not. He was becoming a shell of the child she gave birth to. Herein lies a potential solution to all the school-related violence in the country, if not the world.

Sources

1. "Who was 'Gus' Deeds?" Posted 6:40 pm, November 19, 2013, by Mark Holmberg, Updated at 08:34 am, November 20, 2013. Virginia CBS affiliate WTVR.

2. BLS American Time Use Survey, A.C. Nielsen Co. Date Verified: 12.7.2013

3. "How the World Consumes Media—in Charts and Maps. A map of TV and mobile-phone usage looks like a 50-year history of the growth of the global middle class." Derek Thompson, *The Atlantic*. May 28 2014, 5:24 PM ET.

4. Dr. Daniel Amen interview: "The shrink who believes technology will replace the couch." *The Telegraph*. By Sanjiv Bhattacharya. 7:00AM GMT 06 Feb 2013.

Chapter 7

Living With Love

"Every action taken by human beings is based in love or fear, not simply those dealing with relationships. Decisions affecting business, industry, politics, religion, the education of your young, the social agenda of your nations, the economic goals of your society, choices involving war, peace, attack, defense, aggression, submission; determinations to covet or give away, to save or to share, to unite or to divide – every single free choice you ever undertake arises out of one of the only two possible thoughts there are: a thought of love or a thought of fear.

Fear is the energy which contracts, closes down, draws in, runs, hides, hoards, harms.

Love is the energy which expands, opens up, sends out, stays, reveals, shares, heals."

Neale Donald Walsche

Life is a choice. Every time you wake up, you get a choice to go out into the world and greet it – or not. As human beings, we have the ultimate freedom to do as we choose, in every situation, every moment of every day. Even when there are laws or rules in your society, you have the choice to follow them or not.

We currently live in a time of abundance. There are more countries with democratic, free-society principles than ever before. Regardless of what your opinion is of where the government is today and where it's headed, I believe the bottom line is the world is evolving to a state of higher consciousness.

Take the United States, for example, and the long fight thousands put into establishing freedom for people, irrespective of their race or gender. Slavery was abolished in 1865, and though things could definitely be better, nothing is ever perfect. When you consider where things were, we have come a long way. In this county and every Westernized country I am aware of, my wife, who's African-American, can marry a white guy named Jay, and we can have the opportunity to live the life of our dreams.

Together, we have been able to get legally married and celebrate our love by birthing a beautiful, interracial girl. We will have the opportunity to raise her in a society where she doesn't have to worry about choices – or lack thereof – due to her skin color. In fact, I choose to believe due to her unique heritage, she may even have the opportunity for more life experiences, not fewer.

On top of that, my wife and child will have the opportunity to vote. This is a freedom some may take for granted, as it seems so basic to us in this current time space. In fact, at the time of this book's writing, there are still women alive who were living during a time when women were not allowed to vote.

The right to vote, like slavery, was largely the work of multiple grassroots efforts. Women lectured, banded together, broke laws, wrote, marched and practiced patience over many, many years. The movement required people like Ida B. Wells to get out of their comfort zones and create ripples of change that ultimately became tidal waves.

Ida B. Wells was born a slave in 1862. Despite living most of her life "free," she lived in a time when the rights of black people, especially women, were greatly infringed upon. She wrote firsthand accounts of white-on-black lynching and the horrors black people lived through in their first years of freedom.

She became so passionate about not just freedom, but about being treated equally, that she devoted her life to the cause. Did you know seventy-one years before Rosa Parks refused to give up her seat on a bus, giving rise to one of the most important symbols of the civil rights movement, Ida was dragged out of a bus kicking and screaming? Rosa Parks doesn't become Rosa Parks without Ida B. Wells.

Ida eventually fought for women's voting rights, and despite also being subject to racism within suffrage leaders, she formed the first organized women's movement in Chicago. This woman literally went on to fight one battle after another after another. Eventually, when she left the spotlight to focus on being a mother, she was subject to scrutiny for not doing enough.

Susan B. Anthony is widely considered the suffrage leader of the world, and instead of expressing her gratitude for Ida's work, she was critical of this move into the home. Can you imagine being criticized for doing what comes instinctually to a woman? Yet that was how challenging women's rights were in the late 1800s.

My point here is millions of people, ideas, movements and decisions have brought us to where we are today. It is a wonderful life, and it's a free life. Things will and are continuing to get better for us as a collective species. For all the millions of people that helped further civil rights, arguably the most-known leader of the movement was Martin Luther King Jr.

Dr. King's beliefs were rooted in the ideas and principles of non-violence. In the face of fear that I can't imagine, the man stood his ground, patiently, calmly and lovingly to further what he believed in. Insult after insult, setback after setback came his way – on almost a daily basis. Oftentimes, his campaigns and marches teetered on the timing of minutes and what seemed like incredible luck, but the man never lost faith in his love for equality.

This isn't a history lesson on Martin Luther King. Others tell that story better than me. Instead, what is most interesting to me is just how his principles came to him.

It all started when fellow civil-rights activist and trusted advisor Bayard Rustin counseled King to dedicate himself to the principles of non-violence. The man who inspired Rustin was none other than the renowned, peace-loving humanitarian, Mahatma Gandhi.[1]

Gandhi was widely considered the leader of India's freedom movement from Britain in the 1930s. He pushed freedom not with guns, instead by encouraging Indians to do things like boycotting British goods and buying Indian goods instead. Gandhi preached passive resistance, believing violence against the British only provoked a negative, equally violent reaction. His quiet voice was so strong that perceived small acts of economy created ripples that eventually created large, worldwide waves.

In fact, when he was imprisoned several times from 1922-1940, the British government had no choice but to free him because of the peaceful protests his captivity inspired. Gandhi took his mission one step further, no longer protesting with just words. Instead, he protested by not eating. His call to die of starvation would have painted Britain as a government dictatorship at a time when global tensions were sky high. Britain was a leader during that period for eliminating overbearing Communist or dictatorship governments. It could not afford to have innocent blood on its hands. The world had to listen to the diminutive, albeit powerful, Indian man.

After reading about Gandhi's successes in India, King was called to visit his home nation for inspiration despite Gandhi's death a decade prior. The visit deepened his understanding of non-violent resistance and allowed him to re-create his vision to further American civil rights. By way of radio transmission from India, King furthered his inspiration by stating: "Since being in India, I am more convinced than ever before that the method of nonviolent resistance is the most potent weapon available to oppressed people in their struggle for justice and human dignity."

What shouldn't get lost in the shuffle were the people who made his trip to India possible: the Quakers. The Quakers, a Christian-based religion, were largely comprised of white members and believed in many things that were considered radical at this time in history. One of the more notably radical beliefs widely held by the Quakers was their support for the civil rights movement. What speaks louder than a group of white religious leaders sending a black leader to learn about the man who epitomized non-violent protest?

History can and will be made every day. With the help of those before us, we can stand on the shoulders of giants. One of my favorite quotes is from a personal hero, the developer of chiropractic, Dr. B.J. Palmer. He sums up the whole shebang: "You never know how far reaching something you think, say or do today will affect the lives of millions tomorrow."

These are beautiful words, perhaps the most inspiring words I have ever read, because it means we all make a difference. If we can all make a difference and create change in our lives and in others, then there is just one decision to make: Love or fear?

I select love. Just as Gandhi did, just as Ida B. Wells did, just as Martin Luther King and countless others before me. I select love.

But can life really be this simple?

In the book A Course in Miracles, the Foundation for Inner Peace furthers the case for love more simply: "Every act is either a cry for love or an act of love." A cry for love is explained as a fear-based decision. Oftentimes – and hindsight is always perfect, – we make a decision because we are afraid of someone or something. We are afraid we will get hurt or fearful to hurt someone else. This all serves nobody.

Ever watch one of those romantic movies with Matthew McConaughey? You know the type: my wife loves to watch these movies and I need an adult beverage to make it to the finish. The plot is a love story, but nearly the whole movie features the guy and girl both walking on eggshells, afraid of what the other may or may not say. I want to yell at the screen with these movies and tell McConaughey, "Hey smart guy, she loves you, just be honest with her and tell her you love her!"

They almost always have a predictable, happy ending, and the couple manages to figure it out in the end. But did the guy really need to move to Louisiana to get away from the girl before they got together to begin with? Why didn't he just water the love plant? Just saying … Choose the emotion that goes in the love category and save yourself all the time and anguish, pal. I digress.

If we choose to accept this most simple and basic premise of life, then it should also make our conversation around violence just as simple. But this concept isn't always easy to process or accept – at least initially that was the case for me. So let's revisit the whole act of love vs. cry for love categories.

Acts of Love include – but certainly are not limited to – peace, patience, forgiveness, freedom, civility, honestly, openness, random acts of kindness, exercise, thoughtfulness, forgiveness, introspection, humility, authenticity, sharing, giving without expecting and integrity.

Cries for Love include, of course, fear. However, throw in greed, gluttony, malice, hate, aggression, giving with expectations, stealing, insulting, not sharing, sarcasm, keeping secrets, gossip (a very big one nowadays), cliques, bullying, cheating, and of course, violence.

This is by no means an exhaustive list, just one I wrote down while on vacation at the beach re-creating my soul. My challenge to you: give yourself a thought, word or deed and not place it in one of the two categories. It's impossible. If you don't know which category your human experience goes into, then I suggest a few remedies:

Give yourself permission to be honest. It is so easy to not understand what a thought/word/deed (experience) actually means to you and those around you. And friends, that's okay! Not knowing what you're feeling and not being able to identify with it is part of being alive. Ask me how I know. The challenge is being honest with yourself when you don't know what's going on.

Being able to stop right in your tracks, take a timeout and ask: "What's really going on here?" is a wonderful gift. Few people I know have mastered it, and my wife would tell you I am in the infancy stage myself.

Start thinking about similar words that could describe a given situation. For instance, ignorance is almost always fear-driven, whereas knowledge is almost always love-driven. If you find yourself uneducated on a topic, it's up to you to decide if it's ignorance or dearth of knowledge. Your response to the situation is really what dictates the experience. Will you seek to learn more or go on with the infamous "ignorance is bliss" mindset?

Consider you are having a chat with your significant other about taking the trash out last night. Instead of being 100 percent honest with them, you are being, let's just say, 60 percent honest, when you say, "Yeah, I took care of it." Your intention is you will take the trash out on your way to work and they will never know you forgot. This clearly fits into the cry for love department. Whether it's fear you are going get your ass kicked for not taking out the trash like you said you would or you were just lazy, you have spoken with dishonesty and haven't had integrity with your word.

If your spouse is like my wife, they are going to find out and you will pay the price. The similar words for "almost honest" in this example would be forgetful, lazy, dishonest or ignorant. Make sense?

Employ an accountability partner. What you might consider is asking someone, like a family member, friend or spouse to be an accountability partner for you. Better to have a loving voice stop you than a thousand-pound gorilla.

My intention is not to write a book about God, although it's on my bucket list. However, I do believe in things that are more powerful and more knowledgeable in the universe than me. I refer to this universal force that is continually giving power to everyone and everything God. I know God to have a unique way of slowing me down to start paying attention.

For instance, in the book The Art of Learning by Josh Waitzkin, he tells the story of a woman who was crossing the street in New York City and didn't have the good fortune of an accountability partner. As the story goes, a speeding cyclist nearly ran into a nameless woman. At the last second, as so often happens in New York, the cyclist weaved right around with nothing but a slight bump. Instead of the woman taking inventory, looking around and taking a step back, she got worked into a tizzy and started yelling at the now long-past biker.

I'm guessing you know what happens next: The woman gets belted by a taxi and thrown ten feet into the air, likely to a quick death. No way did this need to happen to the young woman. What would have been ideal is to have had a friend to pull her back off the street and say, "Hey sister, what are you really upset about?" The woman was crying for love, but what did she expect from another nameless biker in a city that is constantly moving?

It may be challenging to listen to the subtle messages that are around us each and every moment of every day. However, your accountability partners, (coming in the form of loved ones, coaches and friends) double the listening power and help strengthen your inner attunement with God as a result.

Back to the two basic categories: A naysayer may state, "Well, I just burped, which category does that fit into?" That depends on your intent. Perhaps you are a young child and deep down, you are a little bit upset your mom didn't buy you an ice cream cone at the zoo. Recalling how your mother once told you a young gentleman doesn't burp in public, you decide to let out a malicious burp after stopping for a drink at the water fountain.

All of a sudden you have your mother's attention. Though she is upset, at least she is again paying you the attention you think you deserve. This simple act of a human bodily function, which is most often preventable, was done out of anger – a.k.a. fear – by the little boy. Fear that your mom didn't love you enough to buy you ice cream, fear that you aren't having enough attention paid to you or fear that there isn't enough ice cream in the world.

The flipside of the childish burp scenario is perhaps you just burped because you swallowed wrong, caught some air and were physically uncomfortable. This fits into the "Act of Love" category, simply because you love yourself enough to be comfortable. You don't care who hears you or what others may think, you love yourself enough to be heard in public or private. It was better to burp than have the hiccups or an upset stomach.

Oftentimes, actions are taken without consideration for why they were performed. I maintain separation from thought is separation from love. An act performed without love also fits into the cry for love/fear category. The public burp or other embarrassing events (we all accidentally do them) are based on perspective. In some cultures, it's understood if dinner was good, a loud burp is most welcome and expected. In our current culture in the U.S., burping at a dinner party is most unwelcome and not appreciated. Again, it's all a matter of your intent.

When we begin to look at life in the fear/love paradigm, we begin to see the beauty in all of life and clarity in death. I maintain that gun violence, especially in the settings of schools, is very clearly a screaming cry for love, for people living in fear. I believe if our conversation is not centered on guns killing people, but rather people killing people, we can talk about real solutions.

Source

Bennett, Scott H. (2003). "Radical Pacifism: The War Resisters League and Gandhian Nonviolence in America," 1915–1963. Syracuse University Press. p. 217. ISBN 0-81563003-4.

Chapter 8

Acausal History

For as long as I can remember, the conversation around shooting violence has centered on the weapon of choice, in this case guns. When a stabbing occurs, as happened in April of 2014 when a 16-year-old male pulled out two knives in a high school, wounding twenty-two, there was no outcry for banning knives in America. Or vice versa, there wasn't a conversation making sure every American has a knife on hand. Why is this?

I believe it's because guns are so polarizing for Americans. Why has this issue become so polarizing? Earlier, we talked about Michael Moore and his documentary *Bowling for Columbine*. He was attempting to get to the bottom of that question as well. Part of the criticism of the movie, when it came out in the 1990s, is there wasn't a conclusion, per se.

Moore makes solid cases for a variety of things that are *not* the root cause of the problem. One of these includes mixed-ethnicity families and mixed-race children, which is especially fortunate for my peace-loving, mixed-race family! Another root nixed as a root is current U.S. legislation and/or what could be called the USA's "violent history." Nope, these aren't considered the root problem either.

To that end, Moore has the viewer consider that countries like Germany have a significantly more violent history and that Canada has similar laws, yet both of these countries have dramatically fewer gun-related deaths. He also notes every country in the world has the same access to the music we have access to, and this is even truer in today's age of internet and smartphones. Then, that famous quote: "No gun ever killed a human, only humans kill humans." Thus, he axes owning a gun as a cause.

I agree with his hypothesis that these are not reasons for where we are today. Toward the end of the movie, he does bring up an interesting proposition: In the U.S., we generally have a culture centered on fear. Fear can be seen on TV, in advertising, on the news, in the home and in your neighborhood.

For effect, Moore walks door to door in Canada just to show the viewer there is so little fear there that people don't lock their doors. It's true; unless you live in the deep rural parts of the country, people in the U.S. generally lock their front doors. The most surprising part for me was not that the front doors were unlocked, but just how jovial Canadians were when Moore and a camera crew walked in. Although there may have been a "get out of here" at some point, it was never shown on tape!

Moore is right: fear is huge. Look around and you will see much of our calls to action in this country center around negative ideas. The ideas don't always but are more frequently drifting toward, "If you don't do this, then be fearful that something bad may happen." Everything from toothpaste commercials (be fearful of bad breath), to insurance companies (you have a dream, but if you don't protect it, why bother?) to stock-brokers (are you prepared for the next economic collapse?) have us locking up our lives! It gets worse. Much of the fear culture revolves around fear for the next generation: our children and our children's children. Thus, the sins of the father become the sins of the daughter, so to speak.

Bowling for Columbine was a bit *60 Minutes*-ish in that it didn't give any tangible solutions. But it brought to light huge problems and the idea that we are asking the wrong questions. If you choose to accept we have been asking the wrong questions and instead center our conversation on love, is there a precedent for this actually working?

Yes, non-violence and love works! It brought independence to India through Gandhi's leadership, which furthered the civil rights movement with people like Martin Luther King, and then spread to other leaders like Ida B. Wells, turning millions of women into voters, and colored women into leaders. An idea can spread quicker and last longer with love and peace than any fear-based message. An act of love always trumps a cry for love. History says so!

Gun violence may be a different topic, but is it any less powerful or large than a nation's freedom or voting rights? Not necessarily, but without agreement about what the root cause of the problem is, it has been historically more complicated. The cry for civil rights, independence and voting rights all centered on essentially one idea: Love and equal rights. Can the conversation on guns focus similarly? I see no reason why not.

Let's assume for a moment that the world gets on board with the idea of fear/love being the root cause of violence in the U.S. Just how viable is it for solutions to seemingly appear out of thin air? Real-life solutions do come easier when you start asking different questions that at one time may have appeared to be acausal. This is also known as outside the box or non-linear thinking.

The most interesting and perhaps well-known source for acausality is the book *Freakonomics* by Levitt and Dubner. These two men wanted to examine the sharp drop in the United States crime rate during the 1990s. If you are unfamiliar with the book or the 1990s crime rate drop, what you need to know is the crime rate fell statistically more in the early nineties than at any other moment in our history.

Today, lawmakers look to stop terrorism abroad and at home. This is a well-documented call to action for voters and politicians. That same call to action was almost exactly how people looked at domestic crime back in the 1980s and 1990s. It's not so much of an issue now because it's largely under control.

Even the president of the United States, Ronald Reagan, was engaged in "The war on crime." Finally, success was achieved, and it almost seemed to happen out of the blue. Yet there were factors that were commonly attributed to this drop. Everything from better policing, stiffer gun laws, financial shifts in government appropriations and an aging population were all listed as factors that created the perfect solution to the escalating crime rate.

These men concluded via scientific study that crime fell largely due to the Roe vs. Wade decision that legalized abortion two decades earlier. Their initial logic was this: Unwanted children are more likely to grow up to become criminals; legalized abortion leads to less unwantedness; therefore, abortion leads to less crime. Their hypothesis has been backed by statically relevant data that has, at least to date, stood the test of time.

I know, could I pick another hotly debated topic to bring into the conversation on the already hotly debated gun debate? Sorry friends, but my intention is to support neither side on the pro-life/pro-choice debate. Instead,

I merely wish to focus on the facts these two men brought to the national stage in 2005. Their research has been under heavy fire since it first came out, largely by pro-life advocates. Yet time and again, they revise their studies and algorithms and the results are always the same: legalized abortion has affected crime rates in a positive way.

How? This was their hypothesis: eighteen years after Roe vs. Wade, the crime rate... [fell] as an entire generation came of age minus the children whose mothers had not wanted to bring a child into the world.

To support this hypothesis, the authors pointed out these unborn children would have been either at the peak of their crime-committing years in the 1990s and/or in the demographic of children generally born into underprivileged and often poverty-stricken environments.

Many children who are born unwanted are left with many of the environments already discussed including, but not limited to, challenging family dynamics, violence on TV and in person, frequent video game culture, poor diet, and alcohol or drug abuse. The factors listed by Dr. Amen that create a violent mind were essentially those often present with unwanted children.

Irrespective of what your opinion is about the abortion study and how valid it may or may not be due to personal beliefs around abortion, it's important to examine one thing: The simple idea that it's more likely that a child born to two loving parents with a loving intent will become healthy, happy and a positive influence to others.

I remember gasping out loud when I realized these guys might actually be on to something. Not so much for the crime and abortion link, but more so that I had spent so much of my life thinking linearly. I, for one, started to think about things spatially, looking at other causes and effects in my life. I started to think, "If Leonard hadn't ever been born, would my father still be alive?"

For people who are vehemently opposed to the idea of abortion, I can empathize with you. I don't suggest killing unborn babies as a solution to our country's violent ways. Yet what cannot be denied is that babies born into love, experiencing loving environments, are exponentially more likely to experience and create love in their lives.

It's not even a matter of unwanted versus wanted, but rather loved versus unloved. In the book *Baby Hearts* by Acredolo and Goodwyn, the authors note the importance of loving human interactions from infancy. The authors looked at studies that indicated a baby can become despondent if rejections happen on a daily basis. This means everything from a parent not responding to their crying to not returning a smiling face.

One of their studies demonstrated if you show a baby an unresponsive or sad-faced person at five months old, the baby will recall the same face fifteen months later. Wow, right? Even more shocking is they remembered the sad-faced person with distaste after all that time had passed, even if they were currently cordial. Just think of the impact you are having on your baby if you are arguing with your loved ones in front of them. I know my little girl can hear me subconsciously even while she's sleeping. Study after study has demonstrated this.

Thousands of children a day are adopted or given loving environments with foster care. One of my best friends was adopted, and he is one of the most fascinating people to be around. My suggestion here is that we create loving environments for all humans to spend their childhood years. We were blessed with a beautiful baby girl, and my wife has insisted when we are done biologically conceiving, we adopt another child.

I initially resisted this idea on the basis of, "I don't know what environment that child came from." But as I sit here today writing this, I now understand just how important it is for all humans to have loving environments for all their lives. You can't tell me that as a culture we can't create more loving children. I refuse to accept that. I refuse to accept that killing a fetus is better than creating a space to love that child. It hasn't always been there, but this can be our reality.

Is there credence to the link between unwanted children and crime stats? Yes. However, I would choose to frame that conversation as "grew up into loving environments and crime statistics." What kind of study would that look like? Crime drops precipitously as adoptions soar and abortions drop. That is the type of acausal shift I expect from human beings.

The other study I would love to see, although I don't know how you would begin to quantify it, would be a study that links overall world love versus violence. Is this a study that would ever need to be performed? Can't we just anecdotally ask, "What am I doing to create love in the world?" If you can look at your life and each interaction and know you gave that person the best love you have to offer, it makes studies like this seem ridiculous.

The reality is gun violence is here right now. By accepting a dearth of love as the problem, how can we as a country – or world – create more love? What does change look like for our family, our friends and ourselves on a daily basis? What real-life, tangible solutions can corporations big and small get behind?

Love, Not Guns

Chapter 9

Solutions

"Ask yourself whether the dream of heaven and greatness should be waiting for us in our graves – or whether it should be ours here and now and on this earth."

– Ayn Rand

Meditating on the circumstances that led to the end of my father's life, I have chosen to have 100 percent clarity, focusing on how love would have changed history. Breaking out the magic time machine for a ride, let me tell you what I see, in my ideal, about what *could* have changed events to benefit everyone. This could serve as a model for all violent events, not just guns or school-related violence.

Let's start with the assumption that Leonard was still expelled from school. That begins our conversation at that point in 1991 – even though we could also put a different storyline together involving Leonard finishing school and graduating with his classmates.

Focusing on the family aspect, one of the causal patterns we talked about for creating a violent mind was challenging family dynamics. After expulsion from school, Leonard's parents, siblings or any extended family would take a deliberate and active interest in his environment; i.e. they start asking the question, "How can we ensure Leonard has the chance to experience a full education?" or "What are my son's (grandson's, nephew's, etc.) life ambitions?"

Clearly, changes to his academic program would be in order. Regardless of whether or not Leonard wanted to work more challenging, higher-responsibility jobs with better wages, earning a high school degree or equivalent would be a worthy accomplishment. At the same time, just because somebody does not have a high school degree or chooses to continue down an alternative road with respect to their education does not mean that person need spend the rest of their life with a minimum-wage job – at least not if he would choose otherwise. Not even close.

Henry Ford, the inventor of the modern car, was famous not for what he knew, but with whom he associated and what *they* knew. Did Henry Ford know how many feet are in a mile? Nope. But at the push of a button, he could summon someone who did; thus, keeping in his head only the information vital to his cause and his passion. Mr. Ford is quoted as saying: "Failure is simply the opportunity to begin again, this time more intelligently." Another favorite of mine from Mr. Ford is also applicable to our story: "Anyone who stops learning is old, whether at twenty or eighty. Anyone who keeps learning stays young. The greatest thing in life is to keep your mind young."

When I went back and researched what Leonard was doing for the two years after being expelled, all I could find was that he worked at several different locations washing dishes. Again, absolutely nothing wrong with washing dishes, although that was probably not his life plan. I know if my children were washing dishes for nearly three years without pursuing an education or more fulfilling career, we would have lots of dialogue about their passions and whether washing dishes aligned with following their bliss.

When it comes to choosing a career path, I believe author James Campbell got it right. Many of his books have the same theme, but my favorite is *The Power of Myth*, in which he tackles the topic of work eloquently: "If you do follow your bliss, you put yourself on a kind of track that has been there all the while, waiting for you, and the life that you ought to be living is the one you are living. Follow your bliss and don't be afraid, and doors will open where you didn't know they were going to be."

Campbell is right. When you follow your bliss, life becomes an authentic expression of who you are. Your life isn't about working less or punching a clock or working for a 401(k). Instead, your life is about following and pursuing your life's passion. For me, that bliss is defined as making meaningful connections with other people around the world, to be a healer and communicator of universal love.

Rather than make assumptions, I wrote Leonard directly and asked for his input on what his plans were back in the 1990s.

My aunt, who I referenced earlier and works in the Wisconsin penal system, told me how I could look up his name and find his current mailing address. Sure enough, she was right, and again, Google works wonders. Perhaps a bit too wondrous, as you can actually see current photographs of the incarcerated. I was very much not ready for the reality of seeing Leonard's face when I sat in my office on a cold December afternoon. But there it was, and still is today.

I spoke with all my mentors and loved ones: Gary, Dr. Tom, my wife, Mom, my brother, and my editor, Mike. Everybody was supportive, and most thought it was a great idea for the book – and if nothing else – therapeutic for me.

I have learned more about the penal system than I ever thought I would in two lifetimes. For instance, the penal system does not have email. However, you can send snail mail to an inmate. I also learned that if you want to speak to a social worker or professional at a correctional institution, good luck with that needle in a haystack.

In the end, I ended up mailing the following letter to Leonard:

Leonard,

My name is Jay Breitlow and I'm the eldest son of the late Dale Breitlow. I am writing this letter in hopes that you are willing to communicate with me about what happened leading up to Dec. 1st, 1993, and perhaps more depending on what you are comfortable talking about. Currently, I'm in the process of writing a book called *"Love, Not Guns,"* which details the growing trend of violence in schools, and what I see as peaceful, loving, nonviolent and non-gun related solutions.

I am doing this in hopes that it will spark people to look around them to help others and not focus on guns. It's my contention that no gun ever killed anybody, people kill people. And I would like to believe that there is something that could have been done to save my father's life - not just him interacting with you but perhaps friends, family, neighbors, classmates other teachers, etc. My goal with this book is in no way, shape or form to put you down, but to merely to state the facts. The loss of my loved father is still painful to this day, but I'm not mad at you or looking to make you an enemy. Not at all.

I don't know that you ever expected to hear from us, or frankly want to, and I want you to know that I would respect it if you decided to never write me back. I am writing this book telling the story, at least what I can remember about it. Most of my family, including myself, has emotional/mental blocks and nobody can recall exact details of what exactly happened around this time. Perhaps you can offer more insight.

If you are willing to write, just write back to the address below and what you are willing to talk about or not talk about. At that point I would then send back a list of questions for us to have conversation about.

Jay Breitlow

~

For the better part of six weeks, I awaited a response to the letter. I used my chiropractic office as the mailing address, and every time one of the office girls got up to get the mail, I would dreadfully await their return. For days on end, just silence. Then one day, it came.

Fortunately, it was a slower morning where I could read the letter and not let it affect the people I was serving. My wife took over for the rest of the morning's patients. My hands were shaking in a nervous fear of anticipation and I struggled for breath as I opened the letter. I sat in my office chair just holding the letter for a good two minutes. Before reading it, I decided to turn to the end and see if it really was from him. Sure enough, it was Leonard, and I started crying seeing his signature, knowing these were the same hands that took my father's life.

The letter from Leonard McDowell, with grammar, and emphases as he wrote the letter is as follows:

3/6/2014

Mr. Jay Breitlow:

Hello, there's some time to write you because presently I have a few days off from my college studies. I'm terribly sorry for what took place at the high school in '93. It's hoped that, in the future, atonement will be made for you and your family's loss – that's something I will certainly <u>try</u> to do.

I definitely regret the breach of the law that was carried out by this letter's writer. What's a matter with me?! I'm appalled and completely "knocked off my can" that I could have caused people so much pain.

In regard to the wherefore that it happened, like I told the trial court in 1994, on March 1, 1991, Mr. Breitlow called on the telephone the police, and one of them with extremely excessive force fractured my skull? And Mr. Breitlow was <u>with</u> that local government employee who committed said crime against me? And that was eating me up <u>at that time</u>, what took place on March 1, 1991, at Wauwatosa West High School.

Obviously it's horrific to no longer have a family member alive but its still, the laws of this country say you're supposed to get a fair trial? I've been behind bars for a good 18 years now, the sentence was 91 years (1994-2085), and so whether to say yes or no to the question will I speak any more regarding <u>why</u> I took the law into my own hands – beyond what I wrote in this letter – at this point in time; I would say no.

I've had way too many problems with people saying to the court, what I said at a previous time and/or at another place, what I said to him or her. So just to state it one final time, I really am unable to go into any more detail that what the trial court heard at the trial in 1994, and that was a huge amount.

I know this being said isn't exactly in sync with what you asked, but the Book of the religion that I belong to and that I became a believer in while I was in prison basically says "do unto others what you would have them do unto you". What happened at the high school in '93 would never happen again because I'm a Christian now?

Good luck with the book.
Thank you <u>VERY</u> much for writing.

Yours,
Leonard McDowell

P.S. As a gift for writing me, I'm sending you a principle I learned from a book I read like several years ago. Here it is: ANYBODY can wish for riches, and most people do, but only a few know that a definite plan, plus a burning desire for wealth, are the only dependable means of accumulating wealth.

~

Thankfully, the letter was not filled with spite, malice or violence. I think this was my worst fear when I first sat down. This gave me an unusual sort of peace, almost like my family and I are safe and I didn't stir up a hornets nest. The letter also makes it pretty clear that the man's diagnosis of schizophrenia is still likely in place today. Having read and re-read the letter dozens of times makes it no clearer what he is exactly trying to say to me.

If nothing else, I find comfort deducing that his mind does not appear to be on my father or our family. He does state clearly that if he could repeat the events of 1993, my father would be alive. There appears to be some undercurrents that he would like to be free now – or perhaps was wrongly tried in court, and these are the only real concerns I could have about the letter. That being said, if I walked past the guy on the street, I have the utmost confidence he wouldn't hurt my family or me.

Not that I am in any hurry for Leonard to get released, but I am glad he is asserting himself. He, in all likelihood, will be in prison for the rest of his life, but that doesn't mean he should accept that he couldn't learn or advance himself.

An interesting aside on how powerful an education truly is was carried out by a study done at UCLA. In the study, the authors noted for every $1 million spent on correctional education, about six hundred crimes are prevented. A correctional education is defined as any structured education received by people incarcerated for crimes committed.

The contrast is the same $1 million invested in incarceration (meaning money spent to actually arrest and jail a human being) prevents three hundred fifty crimes. The short of the study is education is almost twice as cost-effective as a crime-control policy. Talk about more support for love![1]

What is clear about Leonard's letter is he is attempting to gain an education today. He gave no indication as to the nature of his studies. Frankly, it doesn't matter to me what anybody chooses to study as long as they are passionate about the subject. Following their bliss! It gives credence to my assertion that there could have been more challenging and life-enhancing work for him somewhere down the line other than dishwashing.

Education, education, education. This is my first and most basic solution we can provide for the world to reduce violence, be it for our children, our neighbors, the incarcerated, the newborn or the 85-year-old woman in an assisted living center. There is no time or place limit on what we can learn to better ourselves to chase our own unique bliss.

As to Leonard's family situation, I only have the aforementioned information to work with. I have no way of knowing who is alive or how to contact his family today. However, it's not for lack of effort. The basic workings of the McDowell household I know little about. And to that end, what his parents or extended family knew about his life at school or if they were even around to help him during his school years.

As parents, I contend it is our responsibility to guide our children to make decisions that are in their best interest and mutually benefitting to others around them. Clearly, my father was placed in the unenviable position of having a student who was not benefitting others around him, and perhaps he could have altered Leonard's experience to better express love. The details of their relationship are locked up with Leonard.

Leonard speaks in generalities about that specific exchange in 1991, and it seems he harbors even more disdain on the police than he does my father. Likely, had he known those officers, he would have attempted to take their lives first. As to the day in question in 1991, I don't believe when charged with the safety of more than seven hundred students, creating love for Leonard was the first thing on my father's mind. He had a job to do and he did it. And as so many people, students and faculty have attested, he was always fair and loving with those he dealt with. Why would Leonard have been any different? I am certain my father wouldn't have treated Leonard any differently, at least until he became a threat.

Creating loving family dynamics is my second solution for eliminating violence in the world. Largely, this consists of the biological children we traditionally raise in society. As parents, we do have a responsibility to our children to optimize all resources for their growth. This means something as simple as getting young children to bed early to facilitate brain development. It also incorporates more challenging things, like attempting to provide them with tools to excel in primary school and get into college, should they choose that route.

The job of a parent is never done, not even when the child moves out of the house. The exact role of every parent is different, but just asking, "Am I giving my child enough love?" would be a great start and end to every day.

Family dynamics also means creating spaces for foster children and adoptions. The blessing of a child may seem like a curse in unwanted situations, yet that curse for some may be a blessing for others. Can we as a society shift toward a culture that opens our doors more to children instead of alternatives like abortion or raising a child without the love necessary for proper development?

This is a touchy subject, and my goal is not to offend anybody who has a challenging family dynamic or has had an abortion. Nobody can walk a day in your shoes or be subject to the stresses you have. As a young high school student, my girlfriend and I had a "scare" and thought we were pregnant for a week. Not even 18 years old, I can't tell you what we would have done had this been our reality, but at the time I remember thinking an abortion would have been the easiest thing for us.

This clearly would have been a decision that was based in fear. I recall feeling the fear of rejection by peers, fear of judgment that the principal's son (whom the community supported so much) ended up a bad egg, fear of my mother's or family's condemnation… and on and on it went in my head. At the time, young love was real love to me. Would there have been a place for this child in the world? Without question there would have been! What would be awesome would be a world in which we create a shift that everyone knows all children are welcome, somewhere to someone.

Family dynamics also includes divorce. Divorce can be a blessing for parents or a curse, depending on the situation. Parents staying together can be a greater stress than a divorce and vice versa. What is important is to do what is best for everyone involved. The family that stays together only for the children but fights every night over dinner creates just as much challenge as a divorced couple that backstabs the other parent after separation.

Families with limited resources bring up a new set of questions: What resources can our communities make available? Resources include time, money, family, daycare, babysitting and a place to call home. I believe another solution for ending violent minds lies in our connections to community. Even if parents have love for their children and a genuine care for their life, many still don't know what to do or how to achieve some of the aforementioned resources.

Currently, there is very little available cheaply or publicly through the government. However, resources do exist. Church groups or groups of faith offer exceptional youth programs and oftentimes have people who will open up their houses. Almost all churches have a daycare option for children to play and work socially together.

Subtle shifts in our society can open up huge windows of opportunity. In 1993, the internet was not as accessible, well-known or soaked with data as it is now, I will grant you that. However, public libraries and community colleges have many programs available to engage youth. Social media websites – notably Facebook – are hotbeds for bringing together people of similar interests and similar challenges.

Preconception, my wife and I had talked about the challenges of being an interracial family in a predominantly white community. To this day, our community in Colorado has been nothing but welcoming to our daughter and us. At the same time, having the connection to other interracial couples and even being around other African-Americans is very important for my wife.

How have we overcome that barrier? The internet! Meetup.com, as well as Facebook, has helped the two of us meet other culturally diverse families. It is nice to have the exposure to other families with interracial children, and we have found many benefits to the group in addition to support from people with similar challenges.

The common theme with these resources is they do require effort. Just as Andrew Amen had access to incredible resources with locating the cyst in his brain, nothing would have happened without persistence and dedication to love. Recall that Andrew Amen's uncle, Dr. Daniel Amen, just happened to be the leader in brain scanning technology. Yet Dr. Amen still had to overcome innumerable barriers to get treatment for his nephew. If the McDowell family was going through transition such as divorce or deaths in the family, it's conceivable that love wasn't always in the forefront of the household. Where else might change have been found for him?

I believe in the generosity of strangers, and sometimes strange friends, if you will. This is another solution to end violence. Using the idea of a radical shift in consciousness toward looking for the best in people and creating love everywhere, I would see a place in the future where a student or teacher would have noticed that something just wasn't right with Leonard. Perhaps even my father could have taken Leonard under his wing.

That, in itself, may seem a bit odd. But when I think back at people with whom I used to be close or those I may have drifted apart from through the years, or even those wonderful relationships I once had that are now over, I wonder where it all went wrong.

On one occasion in our chiropractic office, we were essentially being threatened with a lawsuit by a former client whom we once had a wonderful relationship. The relationship lasted a year, and despite her having nothing but wonderful things to say to us about her progress, one month after her last adjustment, she called our office demanding a refund, claiming many different things we did were incongruent with how she perceived we ran our business.

Looking back on this experience, it's clear to me this woman was crying for love. Despite our best efforts, as well as those of our entire staff, to make her feel loved and welcomed, she felt the opposite. I can truthfully tell you I have only love in my heart for this woman, despite her malicious attacks on my family and my business.

In the end, I know I did my best to give this woman everything she needed to have an optimal healing experience. Yet, something I did or said to her was perceived as harmful. Sometimes this happens. I read once from noted author Wayne Dyer that he actually seeks out relationships and other people with whom he initially did *not* resonate. He asserts these are the people we have the most to learn from.

He's right! This woman will teach me more about myself and how to communicate with other people than my best friend. If you think about it, how much can you learn about the world from somebody who might be able to finish sentences for you? Best friend support is great, but it's challenges that give strength. Just like muscles, we must be stretched to grow.

How many people do we walk past every day at work or on the street where a simple hello could have changed everything for them? How many people do we know as acquaintances who might be really interesting and have much to offer us? The challenge is to reach out, support and love everyone, even those threatening you.

That doesn't mean I am going to invite this woman back into my office or that my father should have hugged Leonard at gunpoint. Sometimes these people are best loved and supported from afar, through intention and prayer. Love wears many masks and can be presented in many ways.

A couple years ago, there was a series of great commercials run by Liberty Mutual Insurance. They showed people performing random acts of kindness. Each scene lasts about two seconds, and in each scene, you see a third person observing the random act of kindness. Being witness to each act, that third person then is shown in the following scene performing the next random act of kindness. And so it goes.

It's a beautiful commercial that demonstrates how powerful love is. Why couldn't this be a reality today, where someone like Leonard or other violent criminals have their entire lives altered with one random act of kindness? If everyone acted that way and we were each the recipient of a random act of kindness, how would this shift our daily human experience? Thinking more this way very well could have saved me from having to deal with the potential stress of a lawsuit in the office.

This is the communication and shift in consciousness I believe we need, at least in terms of creating a long-term, tangible change in the world toward giving acts of love. We needn't be told what needs to be done or how to help, but we should possess a constantly searching and mindful eye. This may seem very hippie and tree-hugger to some, and I get that, but the idea of love spreads into multiple arenas.

Speaking with as many classmates of Leonard's as I could, I still haven't learned much about who he was. I do not believe he was bullied, but he was clearly an outsider to the "in crowd." Popularity contests and prom dances no doubt weren't his thing. Generally speaking, I don't know of any good that ever came out of prom/homecoming popularity events, although my mother notes that my father was very excited about being homecoming king as "this was a dance to celebrate football."

"We were on prom court, your father and I, but he didn't care about prom," she recalled. "He was all about football."

Whatever your thoughts regarding popularity contests in high school, this much is clear; bullying has never served anybody, ever.

A study in the U.K. found that even fifty years later, the mental and emotional scarring of bullying is still present. That means even as retirement age is approaching, adults are still dealing with the trauma of other children pushing them around in school. Everything from suicidal thoughts to depression and anxiety were reported as still present in daily lives.

Programs that were not in place to support peers in the mid-1990s are now popping up all around the country. A quick Google search for anti-bullying programs brings up many websites with information on them as well as programs for schools, teachers and regular folks alike.

My brother, now a principal at a Wisconsin high school, recently won a contest for best anti-bullying video. You can see it here: https://www.youtube.com/watch?v=WWFboTwAJoQ.

Whether or not Leonard was bullied, he clearly would have benefited from a group or program in which he was included in more social arenas. Awareness, intervention and inclusion in school at all levels are wonderful places to spread love.

Technology is another arena to look for solutions. To date, researchers are still looking for the root cause of breast cancer. Millions of dollars flow into research teams every year around the world. However, we do have a means to detect the disease early in people with the relatively old technology of mammography. The analogy here is I believe we can use brain-scanning technology to look at people individually and optimize brain function.

Much like breast cancer, early detection would be vital. The earlier brain health status is obtained, the easier to make tangible changes. I see a world in which Dr. Amen's work is available in nearly every community, where the solutions for brain health are as well-known as any simple health remedy.

As ridiculous as it may sound, scurvy was once a raging illness for sailing crews. There were problems with routine sea voyages to the Americas as early as the fifteenth century, and caused a swell of problems for countries as recently as World War I. It wasn't until 1932 when a direct link to Vitamin C was determined to be the root cause of scurvy.

What was happening on long sea voyages? Well, due to storage issues (i.e. no refrigeration) it made the storage of fruits and vegetables impossible. People would die by the hundreds onboard. Now, dying at sea due to a dearth of Vitamin C seems unthinkable. Heck, people pay vast sums of money to cruise the ocean and eat daily buffets. That is the beauty of technology, education and evolution. Why can't we evolve to simple truths like this with brain health as well? I see no reason why that can't be our reality.

The simple solution for scurvy was right under people's noses. In fact, about seventy-five years before the scurvy connection was made, the British were adding limes to their water supply to make the stagnant water more palatable. Inadvertently, the Royal Navy had created the healthiest, strongest seamen in the world. Nearly invincible, the best the rest of the world could do in retort was give them a silly nickname. This is why British Royal Navy seamen became known as "limeys." Simple solutions are sometimes found by accident.

Many of Dr. Amen's treatment protocols for brain health are just as simple. In fact, he has found that the bioactive components of Omega-3 fatty acids (fish oil) are deficient in every major psychiatric disorder including depression, bipolar disorder and ADD/ADHD. A simple $20 bottle of fish oil added to the diet often cures these diseases better than a prescription drug – and the only side effect for some people is a little fishy aftertaste.

He's also found two other simple things that should be added to most humans' diets to optimize brain function. The first is a simple multivitamin. The reason for the multivitamin is much like the pre-20th century sailors: we just don't get enough fruits and vegetables in our diet. The second is a very inexpensive herb called Ginkgo biloba, which keeps our brain full of oxygen and staying young. That's it.

Drugs do play a role in brain health as well. It's impossible to take a drug and know 100 percent there will be no side effects or exactly how it will affect you. Psychotropic drugs such as antidepressants, antipsychotics and mood stabilizers impair the ability to accurately and effectively process emotions. Essentially, what these drugs do is take away love by dulling emotion and conscience. In his book *Listening to Prozac*, psychiatrist Peter

Kramer reported his patients on Prozac began to care less, making it easier for them to hurt others.[2]

There is a growing list of mass killings and an association with drugs, especially psychotropic drugs. In nearly every shooting, the gunman was either on a psychotropic drug or recently in a state of withdrawal from a drug at the time of shooting.

Recall Creigh Deeds and his son, Gus. Gus was diagnosed with bipolar disorder and on and off various drugs. Cory Baadsgaard was so heavily drugged when he took twenty-three classmates hostage at a school in Washington that he is said to have no memory of the event itself. Mr. Baadsgaard is currently in prison, but is very active in creating change for drug use on the website DrugAwareness.org. Similarly, there is a growing wave for change at the site www.cchrint.org, which is the Citizens Commission on Human Rights (CCHR) - a non-profit, non-political, non-religious mental health watchdog. According to its website, the CCHR's mission is to eradicate abuses committed under the guise of mental health and enact patient and consumer protections.

Dr. Amen does have the ability to prescribe drugs for brain optimization, but as he discusses in his books, nearly every case can achieve positive outcomes naturally. I share his belief in the power of the human body and the innate ability to heal itself. There certainly may be a need for drugs and surgery in times of emergency. However, you must consider the human mind and how it is being altered both in the short and long term.

Another solution: simply eating dinner together. Dinner and other family-centric bonding events have the potential to eliminate multiple factors that create violent minds. First, consider having dinner at the family table with no television. With the television and video games turned off, you have eliminated two large causes of violent minds. Second, by eating together, you are embracing conversation. The simple act of a family talking engages parent-to-child communication and hopefully promotes everyone into pursuing their bliss; not just the children, but parents as well. The reason many parents go to work is to provide for their children, and dinner may very well reinvigorate this bliss for them.

Ideally, the dinner choice would not be fast food or carry out, but instead a healthy blend of fruits, vegetables and a protein, like fish. This eliminates the dietary stress that causes violent minds. It would really be a victory if the family were to exercise together as well. Just a short stroll together before or after dinner, maybe walking the dog, and a family will have eliminated so many variables that have proven to create negative discourse in the world. It's just that simple! And it's all a shift toward love.

My wife and I do eat healthy and supplement our diets with multivitamins, amino acids and always get organic fruits and vegetables. However, I have a frequently bad habit of taking my iPhone to the dinner table. It's not a conscious thing to do it, and by having the phone at the table, well, I might as well bring a computer. Fortunately for me, I have an accountability partner to help reel me back, check the phone in another room or turn it off completely, allowing us to enjoy our meal together. Mentors and accountability partners are, in my opinion, key to following your bliss and creating a healthy brain.

There are some major gaps in the mental health system in this country. I believe one of the keys to revitalizing the mental health system would be creating fewer violent minds. The old expression "An ounce of prevention is worth a pound in cure," would be applicable here in more ways than one.

First of all, if a violent mind isn't created, it's one less patient. In addition, one less violent criminal event is potentially dozens – if not hundreds or thousands – of people affected. Every time a violent event occurs, people, both directly and indirectly, need to go through the healing process. The trauma, grief and anxiety that comes with these events often takes months, if not years, to recover from, depending on the involvement.

Events such as Columbine, Sandy Hook and Virginia Tech each have a global ripple, touching millions of people. Just because an emotionally affected person wasn't physically there doesn't mean they were not traumatized. I can attest to this as well. I am still healing, and every year on December 1st, other students, faculty and community members remind me they are still healing from my father's murder.

People are mentally ill, and at least by minimizing the numbers, it allows those who are truly sick to get more focused, detailed help. The Deeds family was just one example of thousands that happen every year around this country. But what do you do when the system is flooded and overfunded? What do we do about the 3.5 million untreated schizophrenic or bipolar patients that are currently labeled a "statistic?" We shift our consciousness. We create new tangible changes.

Would Dr. Amen's approach have changed Leonard's mind at the time? Perhaps. Considering the man himself said there has been change in him, a mental health program would have been ideal. It is likely he will always need some professional help, but would that have changed our family and community? Absolutely. Is this a shift toward looking for and creating love? Absolutely. Is it beyond our means? Absolutely not.

Lastly, Leonard was reported by his family and himself to have been a heavy drinker. It cannot be stated enough just how important it is to not poison our minds and bodies. Don't get me wrong, I like a pale ale after work on occasion. I also love a coffee on a cold December morning. However caffeine, alcohol and drugs are all poison and implicated in the creation of violent minds. The thought process behind caffeine and alcohol remains they are okay in moderation. Moderation would be two to three beers a week and a cup of coffee a day. Anything more than that and you are impacting your brain's ability to function – both for the short and long term.

Drugs include over-the-counter (OTC), prescription and recreational drugs. Prescription and OTC drugs exist for a reason, as some people need them to stay alive and others just to get through the day. However, changes in exercise, diet and stress levels will positively affect almost every basic aliment. As a chiropractor, I have seen hundreds of people get off drugs just by taking care of themselves naturally and relieving the nervous system of interference (read chiropractic friends).

Yes, part of this is how you eat, think and move. But did you know the position of the top bone in your neck could lower your blood pressure or reduce headaches? A 2007 study published in the *Journal of Human Hypertension*[3] linked the position of the C1 vertebrae directly to how high or low blood pressure can be. One of the authors of the study, Dr. George Bakris, told WebMD.com: "This procedure has the effect of not one, but two blood-pressure medications given in combination, and it seems to be adverse-event free. We saw no side effects and no problems."

Bakris, who is a medical doctor and director of the University of Chicago hypertension center, oversaw the study. The study found that twenty-five patients with early-stage high blood pressure had significantly lower blood pressure than the same number of similar patients who underwent a sham chiropractic adjustment after two months post-treatment.

I have seen this firsthand when people come into my office with the chief complaint of headache. Lo and behold, after a couple months of treatment, I ask them to measure their blood pressure, just for giggles. Almost invariably, if they had an issue with high blood pressure previously, their levels had dropped to normal or near-normal by this visit. The same bone that is misaligned and causes headaches is also the primary control behind many of our body's functions, including, you guessed it, blood pressure.

Chiropractic also helps with back pain, shoulder pain, hip discomfort and neck pain – you likely have an awareness of this. A $55 adjustment versus a lifetime of Vicodin for back pain? Without even the consideration of the visceral impact drugs take on the body, or without even the consideration of neurologic hygiene, the consistent drug-free life is worth its weight in gold. Yes, we do talk to people about neurologic hygiene just as Dr. Amen talks about brain hygiene and dentists talk about dental hygiene. Just because something is out of sight, doesn't mean it should be out of your mind's view.

A 2014 study also linked the position of that same C1 (the top bone) directly to a 17 percent to 23 percent drop in ADD/ADHD symptoms. This is a relationship very infrequently talked about in the allopathic world. Why is this? Why are we spending billions and billions of dollars on new drugs, which always have side effects, many of them neurologic? Why aren't we spending even a fraction of that money on other natural studies? Why aren't we looking at the benefits of the walnut for example, which is chock full of phytonutrients and natural anti-inflammatory supplements?[3]

Just like all the proposed solutions above, there is no one thing that is going to fix violence. I do have a bias to chiropractic, clearly. Does this mean I think the answer to violence is to just turn off the video games, eat walnuts and get adjusted? No, but do those three things instead of taking a drug for high blood pressure and headaches and boredom, and you will immeasurably move toward health. In fact, just using pain elimination as a guide, know that for millions of people, aches, pains and visceral changes can be brought about by chiropractic, acupuncture and massage. As these are also complementary and natural, they most certainly can be associated with a healthy body and brain.

The solutions are easy and inexpensive, generally speaking. Most are a series of things to-do that bring out the best in you and your family. It costs nothing to take a walk and get outside. In fact, that activity is leaps and bounds cheaper than investing in a TV, couch or movie service. Every couple months you might have to buy a new set of shoes and some outdoor gear, but that's it. Eating healthy food in the house together at dinner costs less than most any prepared meal, even fast food.

Which reminds me, did you see that a fellow in Utah purchased a McDonald's hamburger in 1999 and some fourteen years later, found it in a coat pocket? True story. He found the burger in its nearly new state fourteen years later, looking fresh out of the restaurant. The only thing that was decomposed was the pickle. Apparently there are so many preservatives in the food – if you dare call it that – that it can survive nearly a decade and a half of father time. Seriously, why not eat wood chips instead? Check out http://oldesthamburger.blogspot.com/ for more about the everlasting hamburger, and for more perspective on what this does to your body.

Change, just like happiness, is an inside job. It starts with you, and when you have started to change, it's easy for that change to catch fire around you. Gandhi's famous quote, "Be the change you want to see in the world," liberated a nation. That is all well and good, but I contend it's his modeling that brought about change inside Martin Luther King. In the end, Gandhi was responsible, in some part, for the civil rights movement posthumously.

Don't wait for brain-scanning technology to be an everyday, local occurrence to start educating yourself on brain health. Start looking for family members and children to mentor – or just talk with. This is the backbone of change. Like every other positive movement in the world – all you need is to be driven by love.

Sources

1. "Correctional Education as a Crime Control Program," Audrey Bozos and Jessica Hausman, UCLA School of Public Policy and Social Research, Department of Policy Studies (March 2004) p. 2.

2. ISEPP Statement on the Connection Between Psychotropic Drugs and Mass Murder – International Society for Ethical Psychology and Psychiatry: Statement on the Connection Between Psychotropic Drugs and Mass Murder.

3. *Journal of Human Hypertension* (2007) 21, 347–352. doi:10.1038/sj.jhh.1002133; published online 2 March 2007, "Atlas vertebra realignment and achievement of arterial pressure goal in hypertensive patients: a pilot study," G Bakris, M Dickholtz Sr, et al.

Acknowledgements

I would like to acknowledge my loving wife who has supported me around every turn and pushed me to write this book. Christina is the love and challenge of my life, consistently pushing my capacity to love and learn. Without you, I am a fragment of a human being because my soul yearns to be with you. Thank you, bear!

To my daughter, Selom, who was born in January 2014. There is nothing more motivating than the sound of you waking up next to me while I write. I write this book to create a more loving and complete environment for you to grow into. I write this book as a model for you to ask questions that create more meaningful connections in our world. Never stop seeking and looking for ways to reach out and love!

And to my mother, Sue Breitlow, who has shown that love traverses time and space. The love she has for her husband, my father, continues to this day. Your commitment to family is without bound.

Lastly, to the people who made this book come alive: Dr. Tom Preston, you showed me this answer many years ago and how to ask more pertinent questions. You gave me the light to shine and allowed me to shine without fear; and Mike Dauplaise, Bonnie Groessl and Amy Mrotek at M&B Global Solutions, who not only edited this book, but coached me through the ups and downs of writing from my heart. Without your push, there is no way I am up most every day at 4:30 a.m. making this book come alive.

Love, Not Guns

About the Author

Jay D. Breitlow, D.C., is a former nuclear engineer and pessimist turned optimistic entrepreneur. When not reading, writing or playing in the Colorado Rocky Mountains with his daughter, Selom, Jay focuses his passion on the private chiropractic practice he shares with his wife, Christina.

Jay is driven to help reveal life's authentic nature by creating meaningful connections with people. He believes there are silver linings and teachings that come with every challenge of being human, and all that's needed is a light to show us the path we are walking is divinely perfect. Along with raising children, these challenges can serve as life enhancements that bring out the joy in every thought, word and deed.

In his spare time, Jay enjoys coaching entrepreneurs, real estate, investments and blogging at HappyDadsInc.com.

Made in the USA
Charleston, SC
16 December 2014